Mother Teresa

GREG WATTS

To Suha,
the bestest daughter
in all the world

MOTHER TERESA
Faith in the Darkness

A Lion Book
an imprint of
Lion Hudson plc
Wilkinson House, Jordan Hill Road,
Oxford OX2 8DR, England
www.lionhudson.com
ISBN 978 0 7459 5283 3 (UK)
ISBN 978 0 8254 7870 3 (US)
Distributed by:
UK: Marston Book Services, PO Box 269, Abingdon, Oxon, OX14 4YN
USA: Trafalgar Square Publishing, 814 N. Franklin Street, Chicago, IL 60610
USA Christian Market: Kregel Publications, PO Box 2607, Grand Rapids,
Michigan 49501

First edition 2009
10 9 8 7 6 5 4 3 2 1

Acknowledgments
Every effort has been made to trace and acknowledge copyright holders of all the quotations
included. We apologize for any errors or omissions that may remain, and would ask those
concerned to contact the publishers, who will ensure that full acknowledgment is made in
the future.

A catalogue record for this book is available
from the British Library

Typeset in 10/14pt Photina
Printed and bound in Singapore

Contents

INTRODUCTION

I t's not every day that you receive a phone call from one of the most famous women in the world. It happened to me in 1990 when I was working as a reporter on the Catholic weekly *The Universe*, then based in offices just off Farringdon Road in London. At the time, legislation was going through Parliament to amend the 1967 Abortion Act, and it was looking likely that the time limit for abortions would be reduced from twenty-eight weeks to twenty-four weeks for the majority of terminations. So, in an attempt to impress my editor, I phoned the Missionaries of Charity headquarters in Calcutta and asked to speak to Mother Teresa for a comment.

Since quitting the Sisters of Loreto in 1948 to go it alone in the slums of Calcutta, this pint-sized Albanian nun had become a living saint in the eyes of many. She cared for the dying, was one of the first to care for those with Aids, went to help famine victims in Ethiopia and risked her life to rescue children trapped in a Beirut orphanage in the middle of a civil war. UN secretary-general Javier Pérez de Cuéllar had described her as 'the most powerful woman in the world'. As Kenneth Woodward, *Newsweek*'s religion correspondent, noted, 'Cardinals and bishops glowed in this diminutive woman's presence. When she posed next to Pope John Paul II, as she often did, he was the other person in the photo.'[1] There seemed rarely a week when *The Universe* didn't carry a photo of Mother Teresa, proving that you don't need to be glamorous to sell newspapers.

To my surprise, the Indian sister at the end of the line took my number and said she would pass on the message to Mother Teresa. My phone call was a half-hearted attempt really but I figured it looked good. I told myself that a woman who had won the Nobel Peace Prize wouldn't be bothered to speak to a journalist on a small Catholic paper.

A couple of hours later, one of my colleagues at the far end of the cluttered newsdesk waved a phone in the air and called out excitedly, 'It's for you!'

'Who is it?' I said, still clattering away at my ancient typewriter.

'Mother Teresa!' he blurted out.

If it hadn't been for the look of incredulity across his face, I would have thought it was just another wind-up. It was a rarity for a bishop to return a call in person, let alone someone of Mother Teresa's stature. I remember being incredibly nervous as I took the phone from him. Cupping it to my ear, I heard a faint business-like voice asking me in accented English what it was I wanted.

I don't remember what she said – probably what she always said, that abortion was murder, and it was the greatest threat to peace in the world – but I do remember the headline splashed across the front page that week: 'Mother Teresa speaks to *The Universe*.'

I'm ashamed to admit that I never found Mother Teresa that appealing. She was an extraordinary example of faith in action, but she seemed somewhat one-dimensional and far too holy for someone like me to be able to relate to in any way as I zigzagged along the path of faith. She reminded me of those saints who jump out of the pages of sugary biographies like Catholic versions of Superman or Superwoman.

I wasn't the only one not drawn to her. In a UK television documentary by Channel 4, entitled *Hell's Angel*, journalist Christopher Hitchens had accused her of cosying up to dictators and fraudsters and of running homes where the sick and dying were ill-treated. The image of her as a symbol of compassion was simply a myth created and peddled by the media, he argued. Instead, she was a Catholic fundamentalist and an agent of sinister Vatican foreign policy.

Mother Teresa died in Calcutta of a heart attack in 1997, aged eighty-seven. Just a few days before, Princess Diana had been killed in a car crash in Paris. Two great symbols of the late twentieth century, one of sanctity, the other of celebrity. Only months before, they had been photographed smiling together as they came out of the Missionaries of Charity convent in the Bronx, New York.

In 1998 I found myself in Baghdad, having been invited by the Chaldean Church and the Iraqi government to attend a conference whose aim was to highlight how the UN sanctions were crippling the population. I've never been a great one for conferences. That much Mother Teresa and I did have in common. But by accepting the invitation I would have an opportunity to find out something about what life was like in what was then one of the world's most closed and, we were told, most repressive countries.

I was far more interested in wandering through Baghdad's streets than sitting in the conference hall at the ten-storey Hotel Babylon, where I was also staying, listening to a succession of well-meaning but long-winded speeches by church officials, aid workers and Iraqi politicians.

One sweltering hot afternoon I set off alone through the dusty, broken streets and ended up in Karada, an upmarket district surrounded on two sides by the River Tigris, where many of the city's half a million Christians lived.

Leaving the shops and cafés of the main street, I turned down a

Mother Teresa had visited Iraq just after the Gulf War, and in her matter-of-fact way told Saddam Hussein that she wanted to open a house in Baghdad. The man depicted as a demonic figure by Western governments and media agreed to her request, and soon after a group of her sisters arrived to open an orphanage.

narrow lane, where I came across a small building with a simple sign above the door that said 'Missionaries of Charity'. Mother Teresa had visited Iraq just after the Gulf War, and in her matter-of-fact way told Saddam Hussein that she wanted to open a house in Baghdad. The man depicted as a demonic figure by Western governments and media agreed to her request, and soon after a group of her sisters arrived to open an orphanage.

I rang the bell and a pleasant young Indian sister wearing the Missionaries of Charity trademark blue-trimmed white sari and white veil came to the door. I told her that I was a journalist attending the peace conference. Mother Teresa's sisters are well known for not talking to the media but, after I had explained that I was trying to find out what conditions were like under the UN sanctions and that I wrote for Catholic newspapers, she invited me inside.

She led me down a corridor into a large room, where I was confronted by around twenty-five children. They all seemed to be either physically or mentally disabled, or, in some cases, both. Looking at their innocent faces was heartbreaking. A few were sitting up in cots; others were running around or playing with the sisters. Then I noticed that some of the children were tied to the bars of the cots. I don't know if the sister noticed how stunned I must have looked but she didn't say anything. Instead, handing me a glass of water, she announced to the children that I had come from London. Intrigued by my presence, some of the children crowded around me, giggling and tugging at my hand and asking me questions in Arabic.

When the sister and I sat down in a small room, she explained that some of the children had been abandoned by their parents; in other cases, their parents couldn't be found. It wasn't just the Gulf War that had left many

Iraqi children without one or both parents. In the 1980s the eight-year war between Iraq and Iran had claimed an estimated 400,000 Iraqi lives. Daily life was tough under the sanctions because of shortages of food, medicines and other basics. What's more, there were daily power cuts. When I asked her how the sisters coped looking after a group of children with such serious physical and mental problems, she admitted that it wasn't easy, especially as some of them were hyperactive. The reason why some were sometimes tethered to the cots for short periods was to prevent them hurting themselves, she added. As she talked to me her cheerful expression changed briefly to one of tension and exhaustion. The home was staffed by herself and just four other sisters, all Indian. But her smile soon returned, and somewhere I could hear Mother Teresa's words about accepting hardship, being cheerful and never refusing Jesus. Before I left, the children sang me a song in English. I wanted to cry.

I returned to Baghdad in 2003, a fortnight after US tanks rolled into the city and George Bush proclaimed to the world that Iraq had been liberated. And I went to visit the sisters again. Little had changed. But this time, I wasn't shocked at the sight of some of the children tied to their cots. Some time later, I learned that, because of the bombings, death squads and kidnappings in the city, the orphanage had relocated to the north of Iraq, where it was safer.

As impressed as I was by the dedication of those sisters in Baghdad, I still didn't find Mother Teresa particularly attractive.

This changed in 2007 when Father Brian Kolodiejchuk, the Canadian Missionaries of Charity priest in charge of her cause for canonization, made the decision to publish extracts from her diaries and some of the

While the world assumed that Mother Teresa had a hotline to God, all the time she was, in fact, struggling with feelings of emptiness, dryness in prayer and rejection by God.

letters she had written to her spiritual directors. Some of these writings had been published previously, but I hadn't bothered to read them. This time I did. They were a revelation. While the world assumed that Mother Teresa had a hotline to God, all the time she was, in fact, struggling with feelings of emptiness, dryness in prayer and rejection by God. She spoke all the time about God's love, especially for the poor and the weak, yet privately the word that came easiest to her lips was 'darkness'. As Pope Benedict XVI told a gathering of young people during a question-and-answer session at a prayer vigil in Loreto, Italy, in 2007, 'With all her charity and the power of her faith, Mother Teresa suffered from God's silence.'

While there have been many books written about Mother Teresa, previous biographers did not have these letters available. I hope my book can provide some fresh insights into the life of one of the most extraordinary and controversial women of modern times.

Chapter 1
SEEDS OF FAITH

The city of Skopje lies tucked away in the folds of the Balkans, beneath the slopes of Mount Vodno, on the main route from Belgrade to Athens. Today Skopje is the capital of the Former Yugoslav Republic of Macedonia. Like many places in this backwater of Eastern Europe, it has been shaped down the centuries by an explosive mixture of races and religions: Romans, Slavs, Byzantines, Bulgars, Serbs, Slovenes and Croats. The Mustapha Pasha Mosque and Kale fortress, which stand on hills above the city, are a reminder that for 500 years it was part of the Turkish Ottoman Empire. Its often violent history is due, in part, to it standing on a religious fault line, which opened up in the eleventh century when the Latin-speaking bishops in the West and the Greek-speaking bishops in the East fell out with each other and went their separate ways, splitting the church into Catholic and Orthodox.

On 26 August 1910, when Agnes Gonxha Bojaxhiu was born, Skopje was still under Turkish rule. Her parents, Nikola and Dranafile, were both Albanian and settled there after leaving the historic city of Prizren in what is now Kosovo. Why they left their homeland is unclear. It might have been because of the cholera outbreak in Prizren, or because of Turkish persecution. Alternatively, it could have been because her father saw better job opportunities in Skopje. Agnes, known as

Skopje, Macedonia, shaped down the centuries by many races.

Gonxha (pronounced 'Gohn-jah'), was the youngest of their children. They also had a son, Lazar, and another daughter, Aga.

The Bojaxhius lived on the south side of the River Vardar, in the same street as the parish church of the Sacred Heart, where Agnes was baptized the day after her birth. As a Catholic family, they were part of a tiny minority in a city where the majority of the population were either Muslims or Orthodox Christians.

Despite the countless books and articles that have been written about Mother Teresa, not a great deal is known about her childhood, and what information we do have is sometimes contradictory. She seemed reluctant to go into detail about it with any of the biographers with whom she cooperated. This seems to be less a matter of her having anything to hide or to be ashamed of, but rather that she didn't consider it that important. She always urged anyone writing about her life to start with the birth of the Missionaries of Charity, which she seemed to count as a kind of spiritual year zero.

Agnes was a small child and, by all accounts, not a very strong one, suffering from malaria, whooping cough and club foot. This might be why her parents joined other local families to holiday in Vrnjacka Banja, a pretty spa town nestling amidst woods and rolling hills.

Her father was a bit of a wheeler-dealer. He first worked with a local doctor, selling medicines to pharmacies, before going into business with a builder and then with an Italian merchant who sold goods such as oil, sugar, cloth, leather and food. He may also have done business in the narrow cobbled streets of the city's bustling bazaar, where, five times a day, the chimes of the Clock Tower would have reminded Muslim traders to pray.

While her parents were not wealthy, they seem to have been comfortably

off and generous towards those in need. Their door was always open, and those who came in never left empty-handed. When Agnes asked who these people were, her mother would reply, 'Some are relatives, but all of them are our people.' Another time, she said, 'When you do good, do it unobtrusively, as if you are tossing a pebble into the sea.' Agnes sometimes accompanied her mother when she went to clean the house of an elderly woman, or visit another woman who was an alcoholic. Her father once said, 'My daughter, never take a morsel of food that you are not prepared to share with others.'[1]

Her parents tried to create a home built on the values their Catholic faith taught them. Each evening, the children knelt with them in the living room to recite the rosary, something that left a deep impression on Agnes. On her travels, Mother Teresa never tired of repeating the mantra 'The family that prays together stays together.' This example of deep faith and Christian living left an indelible mark on her.

Years later, her brother Lazar said, 'Of the three of us, she was the only one who did not steal the jam. However, being generous and kind-hearted, she would help me in the dining room to pull open the drawer of the cupboard high up against the wall because I could not manage it myself.'[2]

Her father was a city councillor – the only Catholic – and was involved in the building of Skopje's first theatre. His prominence in the city meant that there were always various local dignitaries, including the archbishop, popping in and out of the house.

While her father was full of life, liking nothing more than an evening

An illustration from a French
magazine of a cameramen
under fire while filming an
engagement during the
First Balkan War, 1912-
1913. The forces of the
Balkan League succeeded in
overthrowing the repressive
rule of the Ottoman Turks.

The Archduke Franz Ferdinand and his wife on a visit to Sarajevo, 28 June 1914. A few minutes later, both would be assassinated. The event triggered the outbreak of the First World War.

filled with laughter and music (he played in a band named The Voice of the Mountains), he was firm with his children, setting clear boundaries, emphasizing the importance of good manners and instilling in them the need for hard work. He believed that their education held the key to their future lives.

Moreover, he was also a fervent supporter of Albanian nationalism, which had been growing since the nineteenth century. When the combined forces of Serbia, Greece, Bulgaria and Montenegro ended Turkish rule in 1912, he hosted a party, setting light to a pile of matchboxes to symbolize victory. His joy was short-lived when, the following year, Bulgaria began squabbling over the spoils and turned on its former allies. The volatility of the Balkans led to the assassination of Archduke Franz Ferdinand in Sarajevo in 1914, an event that plunged Europe into full-scale war.

In 1918, at the age of eight, Agnes's childhood was shattered. Her father arrived home from a political meeting in Belgrade feeling ill and he was rushed to hospital where he underwent an emergency operation. The following day he died.

The large crowds that turned out in the city for his funeral reflected his popularity in Skopje. Whether or not he had been poisoned by political opponents, as some have suggested, cannot be proven.

Her mother now found herself alone and struggling to provide for her three children. It seems that Nikola's business partner took all the assets, leaving her nothing. Although her family owned property and land in Albania, some sort of dispute meant that she was unable to benefit financially. To make ends meet, Nikola turned her hand to sewing and embroidery, making wedding dresses and clothes for festivals.

Agnes completed her primary education at the school attached to the Sacred Heart Church and was then sent to Skopje Gymnasium, a state secondary school. Unlike at home, where she spoke Albanian, lessons were taught in Serbo-Croat. She was an artistic and bright child who enjoyed playing the mandolin and writing poetry. She even had a couple of articles published in a local newspaper. Both she and her sister were members of the church choir and often performed in charity concerts.

FINDING HER VOCATION

At the age of twelve, Agnes contemplated becoming a nun when she had finished her education, but she then changed her mind, thinking she would train as a teacher. The arrival in the parish in 1924 of Father Franjo Jambrekovich was to have a profound effect on her.

Unlike Father Zadrima, his predecessor, he was a charismatic and inspiring priest, brimming with ideas and eager to tap into the energy and enthusiasm of local Catholic teenagers. Agnes joined the Solidarity of Mary, a group of girls who met to pray and undertake good works, and she also took part in organized walks, concerts, outings and other activities.

Father Jambrekovich encouraged his parishioners to pray for missionaries. Agnes became fascinated by missionaries, particularly by the stories she read in Catholic magazines of Croatian and Slovenian priests working in India. When Father Jambrekovich arranged for missionaries to give talks in the church, she would sit there enthralled. At this time, there was great emphasis in the Church on the need for Catholic missionaries. In his 1926 encyclical *Rerum Ecclesiae* ('On Catholic Missions') Pope Pius XI had called for a renewal of missionary activity throughout the world.

Thérèse Martin as a
Carmelite novice in
the nunnery at Lisieux,
circa 1890. She found
God in the ordinariness
of life.

Someone else who fascinated her was Thérèse Martin, a young Carmelite nun who had entered a convent in Lisieux, in northern France, at the age of fifteen and died of tuberculosis in 1897, aged twenty-four. On the face of it, her life was unremarkable. But when her autobiography, *The Story of a Soul*, was published the following year, it became a best-seller. Its appeal was due to what Thérèse called her 'little way of holiness'; in other words, finding God in the humdrum moments of life. What also struck a chord with Catholics was her description of spiritual darkness and feelings of being abandoned by God. She wrote, 'When I sing of the happiness of heaven, of the eternal possession of God, I feel no joy in this for I simply sing what I want to believe.'[3]

She was canonized by Pope Pius XI in 1925 and referred to from then on as St Thérèse of Lisieux, or occasionally 'The Little Flower', a title she sometimes used to describe herself. Despite opting to live a cloistered life, she had always wanted to be a missionary. It was because of this that Pope Pius XI named St Thérèse, along with the Spanish Jesuit St Francis Xavier, co-patron of the foreign missions.

At the age of eighteen, Agnes found herself thinking again of religious life, but more specifically of becoming a missionary. Although her mother reacted to the news with mixed feelings, she nevertheless didn't put any obstacles in her way.

On the Feast of the Assumption in August 1928, Agnes visited the

Catholic shrine of the Black Madonna, overlooking the village of Letnice in the Black Mountains.

Returning to Skopje, she concluded that God was indeed calling her to religious life. She applied to the Order of Loreto, who taught in schools in India. In a brief letter to the mother superior in Dublin, she wrote, 'Be so kind to hear my sincere desire. I want to join your Society, so that one day I may become a missionary sister, and work for Jesus who died for us all.'[4]

The mother superior wrote back, agreeing to accept her, but explaining that before entering the novitiate in Darjeeling in India, she would first have to go to Dublin to learn English.

Her brother, Lazar, who was now an officer in the army, urged her to think carefully about her decision. Agnes replied curtly, 'You think you are important because you are an officer serving a king of two million subjects. But I am serving the King of the whole world! Which of us do you think is in the better place?'[5]

On 25 September 1928, family and friends crowded onto the platform at Skopje station to see her off. Her mother and sister travelled with her to Zagreb, where she had arranged to meet another young woman who was also joining the Loreto Order.

Her departure was noted in the magazine *Catholic Missions*, which commented, 'She was the life and soul of the Catholic girls' activities and the church choir, and it was generally acknowledged that her departure would leave an enormous gap.'

It would be many years before she was to return to Skopje.

Chapter 2
THE MESSAGE

The Loreto Sisters were a branch of the Institute of the Blessed Virgin Mary (IBVM), which was founded by an Englishwoman named Mary Ward in 1609. She saw the new order as a female version of the Jesuits, the Catholic Church's shock troops of the Reformation, who were centuries later to play such an influential part in Agnes's life in India. Like the Jesuits, the sisters of the IBVM. would not live in an enclosure, would wear ordinary clothes, rather than a religious habit, and would undertake any work they were asked to do. Although her new congregation flourished, Ward aroused the suspicions of some bishops. She was accused of being a heretic and her convents were closed down. When she travelled to Rome to plead her cause before the Pope, she was acquitted of the charge. She died in England in 1645.

The Loreto Sisters were founded by Frances Ball, who left the IBVM convent in York to establish a religious community in her home city of Dublin. She and three other young women moved into Rathfarnham House, which the archbishop of Dublin had given her, and renamed it 'Loreto' after the village in Italy where, according to legend, Jesus' house in Nazareth was miraculously transported. Her community became known as the Loreto Sisters.

In 1841 a group of Loreto Sisters left Ireland for Calcutta, where they started a girls' school. Six years later, they started another school in Darjeeling.

When Agnes walked up the driveway to the imposing Loreto Abbey, set in its spacious grounds, like any eighteen-year-old facing a new chapter in their life, she must have felt excitement tinged with anxiety.

During her six weeks there, Agnes would hardly have ventured

beyond the abbey gates. Her days would have been spent learning English and helping out with domestic chores. Her real formation would only begin when she entered the convent at Darjeeling to begin her postulancy, a sort of trial period before beginning her proper formation as a novice.

DARJEELING

On 1 December 1928, Agnes set sail on the five-week voyage to India. She got her first glimpse of her strange and exotic new homeland when the ship docked at Madras. She later wrote, 'Many families live in the streets, along the city walls, even in places thronged with people. Day and night they live in the open on mats they have made from large palm leaves – or, often, on bare ground. They are all virtually naked, wearing at best a ragged loincloth. On their arms and legs they wear very thin bracelets, and

She was soon to learn that most people in India held very different religious beliefs to hers.

ornaments in their noses and ears. On their foreheads they have markings, which have a religious significance.'[1]

She was soon to learn that most people in India held very different religious beliefs to hers. Around 80 per cent of Indians were Hindu and ten per cent Muslim. Christians, like Sikhs, Buddhists, Jains, Zoroastrians, Jews and others, were a minority.

Christianity had first arrived in India in the first century – some suggest it was when St Thomas the apostle landed by boat at Cranganore in Kerala on the south-west coast. In 1542 St Francis Xavier, a Spanish Jesuit, spearheaded a Catholic mission to Goa at the request of the king of Portugal. The nineteenth century saw another wave of European missionaries, both Catholic and Protestant, of which the Loreto Sisters were part.

Agnes's new home was a large Victorian convent in Darjeeling, an attractive town set high in the foothills of the snow-capped Himalayas. It had become a popular summer residence with the ruling British classes, seeking to escape the sweltering heat of Calcutta.

After Agnes completed her postulancy, she became a novice in May 1929 and was now clothed in a white habit and black veil. As is usual for a novice, she changed her name, calling herself Mary Teresa, after the Virgin Mary and St Thérèse of Lisieux. The purpose of her novitiate, like any other, was to provide the young nun with the spiritual and practical foundations to live the life that lay before her. In other words, it was an apprenticeship. Daily Mass and communal prayer – the 'Divine Office' – in the morning, at midday, evening and night provided the bedrock. Much of the day would have been spent in silence. Agnes learned about the history of the order and its spirituality and studied the Bible, church doctrine and teaching. As she still only had a rudimentary knowledge of English, she must have found her studies hard.

On 24 May 1931, she knelt in the novitiate chapel and took her first temporary vows of poverty, chastity and obedience. She would renew these annually for the next six years when she would then take her final, or solemn, vows.

As Sister Teresa, she was now ready to be given her first tasks as a fledgling sister, teaching in the convent school and also working with a group of nurses in a mission station. In an article for the magazine *Catholic Missions* in November 1931, she wrote, 'The tiny veranda is always full of the sick, the wretched and the miserable. All eyes are fixed, full of hope, on me. Mothers give me their sick children, their gestures mirroring those in the picture in the pharmacy. My heart beats in happiness: I can continue your work, dear Jesus. I can ease many sorrows. I console them and treat them, repeating the words of the best friend of souls. Some of them I even take to church.'[2]

Many of those who came to the hospital had walked for as long as three hours. Because most of the patients were poorly educated, she often had to explain several times how to take a particular medicine.

She was particularly struck by a picture hanging in the hospital pharmacy. It showed Jesus surrounded

Mother Teresa completed her novitiate at Darjeeling, in the foothills of the Himalayas. Mount Kanchenjunga provides a spectacular backdrop to the town.

by a throng of suffering people. 'Each morning, before I start work, I look at this picture,' she wrote. 'In it is concentrated everything that I feel. I think, "Jesus, it is for you and for these souls." '

CALCUTTA

After completing her two-year novitiate, she packed her few belongings and boarded a train for Calcutta, India's largest city. Situated on the banks of the River Hooghly, spanned by the imposing Hooghly suspension bridge, Calcutta was a vibrant, colourful and chaotic city, with rickshaws, trams, buses, bicycles, taxis and even cattle fighting to get through its teeming streets.

With its palatial Government House, the domes of the Victoria Memorial and the Marble Palace, set in acres of parkland, parts of it seemed to have been transported from England. Behind these images of colonial power, many of those squashed into its tightly packed streets barely eked out an existence.

Sister Teresa's new home was in a pleasant convent compound in Entally, a run-down district in the east of the city, close to Sealdah railway station. The compound contained two schools, one for around 500 girls from well-to-do families and the other, St Mary's, for girls from families of more modest means.

She was assigned to St Mary's, which was run by the Daughters of St Anne, a congregation of Bengali sisters established by the Sisters of Loreto. Instead of the traditional black and white habit they wore blue saris. She first taught history and then geography. From the little we know, she seems to have been a natural and popular teacher. She tried to instil

into the girls an awareness of the needs of those less fortunate. She did this by encouraging them to make small sacrifices for example, by forgoing an outing or doing without sweets and giving the money to the poor, who lived just beyond the convent walls in Moti Jihil, an area sometimes known as the Pearl Lake after the dirty pond in the middle of it, which provided locals with drinking water.

Sister Teresa became involved with the Solidarity of Mary, which was run by Father Julien Henry, the parish priest of her church. It was similar to the group she had been a member of in Skopje. Each Sunday, she went out into the slums of Calcutta to visit the poor, even though she felt that she had little to offer them. She wrote of a visit to one building: 'In that building, twelve families live; each family has a single room, two metres long and a metre and a half wide. The doors are so narrow I can scarcely squeeze through them, the ceilings so low it is impossible to stand erect. And these poor people have to pay four rupees for these hovels; if they do not pay promptly they are thrown out onto the street. I am no longer surprised that my pupils love their schools so much, nor that many are so ill with tuberculosis.

'One poor woman never complained of her poverty. I was sad, and at the same time happy, to see how my arrival gave her joy. Another said to me, "Oh, Ma! Come again – your smile has brought the sun into this house." On

the way home I thought, Oh God, how easy it is to bestow happiness in that place! Give me the strength to be ever the light of their lives, so that I may lead them at last to you.'[3]

In 1937, her long period of formation over, she returned to Darjeeling to make her final vows – her final commitment to life as a nun. Such was the solemnity and importance of the ceremony that it was presided over by Archbishop Ferdinand Perier of Calcutta. Kneeling before him, now dressed in a black habit, black veil and white wimple, and surrounded by the other sisters, she committed herself to serving God as a member of the congregation for the rest of her life. But she was to keep only part of her promise.

Five years later, she decided to take a secret additional vow: never to refuse Jesus anything. It was a vow that was to be the reason for much that she did later in her life.

Her teaching ability and leadership skills were acknowledged when she was made headmistress of St Mary's and also the superior – or head – of the Daughters of St Anne. (Oddly, she only seems to have held this position for a short time before her predecessor, Mother Cenacle, an elderly Mauritian, was reappointed.)

Calcutta was meanwhile experiencing a period of intense pressure. The city's already burgeoning population was further swelled after famine struck Bengal in 1943, claiming an estimated 2 million lives. Tens of thousands of people headed to Calcutta in search of food. Tensions between

Bodies lying in the streets of Calcutta following five days of fighting between Hindus and Muslims in August 1946. Around 3000 people were killed in the violence.

Hindus and Muslims that had been simmering for some time erupted in August 1946 in what later became known as 'The Day of Great Killing'. Four days of rioting and violence brought terror to the streets of Calcutta, leaving an estimated 5,000 people dead and another 15,000 injured.

The chaos meant that supplies of food to the city dried up, leaving the 300 pupils at St Mary's school with nothing to eat. Despite the dangers, Sister Teresa left the school and ventured into the bloody streets. She was stopped by a lorry-load of soldiers and urged to return to the school. She refused, explaining the desperate situation her pupils were in. When they heard this, the soldiers agreed to deliver some bags of rice to the school. This was not the only time she was to put her life on the line for others.

THE CALL

On 10 September 1946, Sister Teresa boarded the crowded overnight train to Darjeeling to make her annual retreat at the Loreto convent. As the endless Calcutta suburbs gave way to countryside, she must have looked forward to the opportunity for prayer and reflection. She was now thirty-six years old and it had been nearly eighteen years since she left Skopje to join the order. While she was happy teaching, she found it hard to forget about all those beyond the convent compound who found it a struggle to survive each day. As a Loreto Sister, she lived simply and frugally but, compared with the poor, her life was one of comfort and ease. She always had three meals a day, clean clothes, a bed to sleep in and no worries about money.

As the train wound its way north towards the peaks of the Himalayas, something happened to her. It was a moment that was to change her life

The incident that changed
Mother Teresa's life occurred on
a train journey to Darjeeling. This
early photograph shows a train
negotiating a precipitous loop on the
line that she would have travelled.

for ever: she felt that she heard God asking her to leave the convent and live among the poor. It was what she was later to describe as a call within a call, saying, 'The message was quite clear: I was to leave the convent and help the poor whilst living among them. It was an order. I knew where I belonged, but I did not know how to get there.'[4]

When she returned to the convent in Entally eight days later, she told some of the other sisters about what had happened on the train. We don't know what their reaction was, but we can assume that some, at least, would not have been convinced by her story.

Sister Teresa's spiritual director was 38-year-old Father Celeste Van Exem, a Belgian Jesuit who had lived for a time in the desert with the Bedouin and was now a priest at Our Lady of Dolours Church. When she told him about hearing the voice and showed him some notes she had scribbled during the retreat in Darjeeling, he listened carefully. His response was to encourage her to pray about it, adding that if she still felt this call in January, he would speak to Archbishop Perier.

A TESTING TIME

Sister Teresa felt an intensity of union with God that she had never experienced before. She had no doubts that

God had spoken to her, and she was impatient to begin her new mission immediately. But as she was to discover, the Catholic Church moves carefully and slowly in such matters. For a professed nun to leave her order is not a simple matter. The commitment Sister Teresa made to the Sisters of Loreto eleven years before was supposed to be for life. To be released from her vows would involve her case being examined by Archbishop Perier, the general superior of the order, and also by the Vatican.

In January 1947, Father Van Exem suggested she write to Archbishop Perier. In a long, passionate letter, she told him that during her retreat at Darjeeling she had heard a voice, which, among other things, had said to her, 'I want Indian nuns' and 'Refuse me not'.[5] The voice went on to say that many street children needed to be saved because they fell into sin every day. And some orders of nuns were ignoring these children, preferring to work with the rich. She set out her plans for the new congregation, 'the Missionaries of Charity' or 'Missionary Sisters of Charity', which included living in poverty, living a life of prayer, running free schools and caring for the sick and dying.

To support her case, she cited the example of St Frances Xavier Cabrini, who in 1880, after being rejected by two religious communities because of her poor health, was encouraged by a bishop to start a new congregation, the Institute of the Missionary Sisters of the Sacred Heart. She started a mission in the US and went on to found a string of hospitals, orphanages and schools, becoming the first US citizen to be canonized.

Despite Sister Teresa's pleadings and talk of a voice, the archbishop was unconvinced that it would be the right thing for her to leave her order. If she wished to work among the poor, then she should do it in conjunction with an order such as the Daughters of St Anne. It seemed to make sense, he said, as they were already doing this work. Why start a new order? And given the tense political and religious climate in the city, he was also concerned that a European nun going among the poor might attract hostility in some quarters. The last thing he wanted was accusations that Catholics were looking to make capital out of the volatile situation. He said he would wait a year before making any decision. This was prudent. His view was if Sister Teresa really did have a calling to leave the convent and work with the poor, then she would feel the same way in a year's time.

She was disappointed and frustrated, but she remained obedient to the archbishop. If it was God's will, then it would happen.

All was not well, though, between her and her Loreto superiors. They had become concerned about her behaviour, not least her relationship with her confessor, Father Van Exem. Some sisters had raised questions about the amount of time she was spending with him. This may have been nothing more than the kind of petty jealousy that sometimes surface in the hothouse atmosphere of religious communities. Whatever the reason, Sister Teresa was packed off to a Loreto convent in Asanol, a mining town north of Calcutta, where she was put to work teaching Hindi, Bengali, hygiene and geography. As superiors of religious congregations were allowed to read all correspondence written by sisters, she thought it wise to stop writing to Father Van Exem.

However, she continued writing to Archbishop Perier, begging him to change his mind and let her start a new community straightaway, referring again to Frances Xavier Cabrini and asking, 'Why can't I do for him [God] in India what she did for him in America?'[6] The letters contained the same sense of urgency that was to characterize her life later on. Each time, however, he insisted she wait. He wanted to be sure that her request wasn't due to self-interest, religious delusion or simply an excuse to quit the Loreto Order.

She countered the increasingly exasperated Archbishop Perier's caution by urging him to write to Pope Pius XII. 'Don't delay,' she said, 'in case souls are lost.' In one letter, Archbishop Perier replied that he was 'rather astonished' by her insistence that he give in to her request. Only the Vatican, he explained, could grant her this permission. He asked her to write down a brief outline of her proposed congregation's aims, means, rules, recruitment methods and possibilities of success. He told her that he was going to Rome for a few months and would look at what she had written when he returned in September.

In May 1947, she left Asanol for Darjeeling to make a retreat at the Loreto convent. Here, according to Father Van Exem, she passed through an 'awful desolation' and was tempted to abandon her plan. But she persisted, sending the archbishop the outline of her plans he had requested. Father Van Exem told her to now forget about the matter and leave it with Archbishop Perier.

Later that year, Britain granted India independence, partitioning it into two states: East and West Pakistan, which was mainly Muslim, and India, which was mainly Hindu. This triggered more violence across the country, setting in motion one of the largest migrations ever seen, with millions of Muslims leaving for Pakistan and millions of Sikhs and Hindus fleeing to India. In one incident, a train travelling from Delhi to Pakistan was ambushed near the Sikh holy city of Amritsar and around 1,200 Muslim refugees were massacred.

Waves of hungry and desperate people flooded into Calcutta. In July, when Sister Teresa returned to the city from Asanol, the sight of so many desperate people on the streets only served to increase her sense of urgency to begin her mission.

In a letter to Father Van Exem, she claimed to have received three visions. In the first, she was in the middle of a crowd who called out, 'Come come, save us – bring us to Jesus.' In the second the Virgin Mary told her, 'Bring them to Jesus – carry Jesus to them.' And in the third, Jesus asked her, 'Will you refuse to do this for me?' Sister Teresa answered, 'You know, Jesus, I am ready to go at a moment's notice.'[7]

It wasn't until 16 January 1948, after he had consulted a theologian in Rome and several trusted priests, that Archbishop Perier decided to give her the permission to follow what she believed to be her call.

He agreed that Sister Teresa could write to Mother General Gertrude Kennedy in Dublin, asking to be released from the congregation. If she consented, permission would then have to be sought from the Vatican, which he knew was not keen on orders duplicating the work of the hundreds of existing female orders.

Father Van Exem agreed to help her draft the letter to Mother

Gertrude, explaining that there were two options: an indult of exclaustration or an indult of secularization. The first would mean that she remained a religious, bound by her vows, and could return to the Loreto Sisters if her venture failed; the second meant that she would no longer be under vows and would become a laywoman. Father Van Exem advised her to apply for exclaustration. He may have felt that this would provide her with some security and a home if her mission failed. But she didn't seek security rather the opposite. She wanted to live like the poor. She ignored his advice and opted for secularization. She was convinced that because God was calling her she would not fail.

Archbishop Perier also favoured secularization. In the covering letter he sent with Sister Teresa's request, he wrote that she 'has not always been understood well and that in the opinion of a few she is not considered very highly, perhaps even not favourably, owing chiefly to her previous education, different in many ways from one imparted in other countries of Europe; she is Yugoslav by nationality' (her homeland was now part of Yugoslavia). Yet he supported her request, describing her as 'entirely oblivious of self'.

Given the tensions Sister Teresa appeared to have with some in the Loreto community, Mother Gertrude might have been expected to turn her request down. But she didn't. She gave her permission to leave the order, advising that she should not apply to the Vatican for secularization, but exclaustration, which would mean that she remained a religious sister.

The volatile atmosphere in the city increased a few days after Mother Gertrude's letter when Mahatma Gandhi, who had led India's struggle for independence from British rule, was assassinated, gunned down as he made

his way to a prayer meeting in New Delhi. Brought up a Hindu, Gandhi looked for what was good in all religions, believing that the only morally acceptable way to bring about change in society was through non-violent means, especially civil disobedience. His most symbolic act occurred in 1930 when he led thousands of his supporters on a 300-mile march – the Salt March – from his ashram near Ahmedabad to the sea to protest against the British tax on salt. His death sparked more riots across the country. India had lost one of its greatest sons, just as the woman who was to become its greatest adopted daughter prepared to begin her mission.

Father Van Exem helped Sister Teresa draft another letter, this time to the Sacred Congregation for Religious in Rome. It was first sent to the archbishop for forwarding to the apostolic nuncio in Delhi, who would then send it in the diplomatic bag to Rome. Archbishop Perier told her that she had been given permission to leave the Loreto Sisters, but only for one year, and she had been granted the indult of exclaustration. After the year was up, it would then be for Archbishop Perier himself – her new superior – to decide her future.

Sister Teresa had decided that she would no longer wear the long black and white habit of the Loreto Sisters, but a simple sari. Pope Pius XI had called for missionaries not to impose their own culture but to adopt the customs and way of life of the people they served. As she already spoke Bengali and Hindi, wearing a sari would not seem as out of place as it might for another European.

On 16 August 1948, wearing a cheap white sari with a blue trim, which she had purchased from a local bazaar, and with just five rupees in her pocket, she joined the crowds boarding the train to Patna, a city on the River Ganges in the north-west of the country. Her plan was to spend four months at the Holy Family Hospital to learn about simple medical care. Leaving the Loreto Sisters, who had been her family for twenty years, was not easy. She had been very happy with them. She was now completely alone.

Chapter 3
SERVING THE POOR

The Holy Family Hospital in Patna was run by the Medical Mission Sisters, a religious congregation consisting of doctors and nurses. It was founded in 1925 by Anna Dengel, a 33-year-old Austrian. After qualifying as a doctor, she went to work in northern India, where she was appalled by how many of the population lacked access to basic medical care. This was a particular problem for Muslim women, who wouldn't allow themselves to be treated by male doctors. The sisters ran not only a hospital in the city but also a nursing college for young Indian women.

Sister Teresa was put through a first aid crash course by Mother Dengel, learning about diseases such as cholera, tuberculosis and smallpox; surgery, midwifery and caring for babies and sick children. She was also taught the importance of hygiene, how to make hospital beds, give injections, administer medicines and deliver babies.

While Sister Teresa's enthusiasm for knowledge and willingness to do anything she was asked impressed the Medical Mission Sisters she worked with, some of her ideas also alarmed them. When she revealed to Mother Dengel that she was planning to give the sisters who would eventually join her diet of only rice and salt, like the poor, Mother Dengel was horrified, telling her that if she did, they would all die. To undertake the kind of work she was planning to do, a nutritious and balanced diet was essential, she explained, as any sisters needed to be strong for such arduous tasks. Furthermore, she went on, because hygiene was crucial, clothes must be washed thoroughly and daily.

During her stay at Patna, Sister Teresa met Jacqueline de Decker, a young Belgian social worker who had come to India to help the poor. When she heard about the work she was to undertake in Calcutta, she asked to join her. However, she was in poor health, and when she returned to Antwerp, she was told that she had a disease of the spine and would have to undergo several operations. Yet she was still to play a part in Sister Teresa's work.

Recalling Sister Teresa's time at the hospital, one Medical Missionary Sister said, 'A few days before she left, Mother Teresa and I had a chat in the garden, our backyard cemetery, among the tombstones. She remarked that she had no idea where or how she was going to proceed with the ideals she had.'[1]

After just a few weeks at Patna, Sister Teresa decided she had learned enough and requested permission to return to Calcutta. She was anxious to begin her mission. Father Van Exem and Archbishop Perier, however, were rightly concerned that she might not have enough medical knowledge to begin such work. Somewhat surprisingly, Mother Dengel supported Sister Teresa. A few weeks hardly seemed adequate preparation for providing medical help to people who would have multiple health problems. Maybe she was caught up in Sister Teresa's enthusiasm to serve the poor. Or maybe she recognized in her the same kind of zeal that had led her to plunge into the unknown and start the Medical Missionary Sisters.

INTO THE SLUMS

Sister Teresa had assumed that she would be able to stay temporarily in an empty property owned by the Loreto Sisters. She was taken aback when the mother general told her that this wasn't possible as it was 'contrary to the customs and spirituality of the institute'. This was not the kind of response

Calcutta's streets were
lined with beggars,
as here outside the
Kalighat Temple.

she had expected from an order to which she had given twenty years of her life. Undaunted, she stayed with the Little Sisters of the Poor in St Joseph's Convent, where they looked after the elderly.

Before beginning her mission, she made an eight-day retreat under the direction of Father Van Exem and entrusted her future to God, confident that he would guide her and provide for her.

Early one morning just before Christmas 1948, she set off from St Joseph's to the ramshackle buildings and huts in the narrow lanes and alleys of Moti Jihil. The partition had brought swarms of desperate people into

Young Indian
women joined
Mother Teresa's
mission to care
for the sick and
the poor.

the city. Everywhere she looked, people lacked food, clothes and medicine. Many had ended up sleeping in railway stations, on the banks of the River Hooghly, on pavements, or anywhere they could find a space. Most survived by begging; others lay in the streets waiting to die. The soup kitchens and dispensaries the city corporation had set up were overwhelmed.

As the only thing she knew how to do was teach, Sister Teresa decided to set up a school in the open air. She knew that there were hundreds or maybe even thousands of children in Moti Jihil who received no education. The fact that she didn't have any desks, chairs or even pencils, or any money to buy them, wasn't going to stop her. God would provide.

It wasn't long before she found families who were more than willing to take up her offer to educate their children. Even so, people must have been somewhat puzzled, even suspicious, by this smiling European woman wearing a simple white sari and cheap sandals.

On the first day of the school, she sat a group of children down on the ground in front of her and began to teach them nursery rhymes and the Bengali alphabet, scratching the letters on the ground with a stick. She also gave them practical lessons in hygiene, showing them how to wash and comb their hair.

Word about her soon spread, and more children began coming each day to her. It wasn't long before she began looking for a property. The five rupees she had left the Loreto convent with were just enough to cover the rent of two small huts.

For nourishment, she gave the children milk at midday and those who attended regularly, paid attention and kept themselves clean, received a bar of soap as a prize. Some years later, she remarked that for some of the children it was probably the first wash they had ever had in their lives.

In the diary she kept at the time, one entry read, 'Met N., who said there was nothing to eat at home. I gave him the fare for my tram, all the money I had, and walked home.'

What must have been at the forefront of her mind was that she only had a year to prove to Archbishop Perier that she had a genuine vocation to live among the poor. If her work was to succeed, then she needed others as committed as she was. So, then, who would be prepared to give their time to provide help and for no money? The answer was some of her former pupils from St Mary's.

One day in 1949, Father Van Exem mentioned to Michael Gomes, a member of the Legion of Mary, which had been founded by Dubliner Frank Duff to undertake work with the poor and disadvantaged, that Sister Teresa needed somewhere to live. Gomes offered the second floor of his three-storey colonial house in Creek Lane, which had been vacant since two of his brothers had left the year before to live in Pakistan. His offer was gratefully accepted.

When Sister Teresa moved in, all she brought with her was a packing case to use as her desk, a suitcase, boxes and a chair. Gomes refused to accept any rent from her.

A few weeks later, Subashini Das, one of her former pupils from St Mary's, turned up at the house in Creek Lane and told Sister Teresa that she wanted to join her. Some time before, Sister Teresa had given evidence in court when her parents had tried to remove Subashini from school to have her married. The following month, Magdalena Gomes (no relation to the family who owned the house) joined, swiftly followed by two more girls. Given that the girls had final examinations to sit, it's perhaps not that surprising that their families didn't share their enthusiasm for helping the poor.

It was not only the girls' families who were unhappy with Sister Teresa. The Loreto superiors saw her as poaching their future novices. Consequently, students were forbidden from having anything to do with her. Some Loreto Sisters even suggested that she was working with the devil.

Sister Teresa began teaching her recruits everything she had learned in the hospital at Patna: how to wash bodies, clean sores, bandage wounds and so on. Nevertheless, she believed her primary job was to help each of them to grow in the love of God and develop a life of prayer. She took them to Mass at St Teresa's Church and arranged for them to have catechetical instruction from Father Van Exem.

When she first thought of setting up a new congregation, during that train journey to Darjeeling, it might not have dawned on her what a huge responsibility she would be taking on. She now had to find some way of providing money, food, clothes and everything else her sisters needed.

Pius XII (1876-1958), pope from 1939 until 1958.

Mother Teresa saw Christ in the poorest of the poor.

If she ever wondered whether she was capable of forming and leading a religious community, then she had only to think of what pioneering women such as Mary Ward and Mother Dengal had managed to do.

Sister Teresa wrote to a friend at the time: 'How much the people here suffer, and how much they need God! And we are so few to help them. If you could see their faces light up when they meet the sisters! Pray to Our Lady to send us more nuns. Even if there were twenty, we should still have plenty of work for all of us here in Calcutta.'[2]

In August 1949 her year of exclaustration expired. It was now up to her superior, Archbishop Perier, to decide her future and that of her sisters.

LETTER TO ROME

For all their good work, Sister Teresa and her band of young women still had no official status in the Catholic Church. They were nothing more than a group of dedicated Christian women. To receive the support and backing of the church, which would be essential for their growth and, crucially, their acceptance by bishops and priests, they needed to become recognized as a religious congregation. This had to be done in accordance with canon law, which stated that a congregation needed to have a constitution, known as a rule. As Sister Teresa knew nothing of canon law, Father Van Exem and Father Julien Henry both helped her draft a document that would meet with approval in Rome.

The rule said: 'Our special mission is to work for the salvation and holiness of the poor. As Jesus was sent by the Father, so he sends us, full of spirit, to proclaim the gospel of love and pity among the poorest of the

LET MY HANDS
HEAL THY
BROKEN BODY

SERVING THE POOR

All along, she was adamant that the work could never become more important than Jesus Christ.

poor throughout the world.' It went on: 'Our special task will be to proclaim Jesus Christ to all people, above all to those who are in our care. We call ourselves Missionaries of Charity.'[3]

Some who set out to help the poor and disadvantaged do so out of humanitarianism, but Sister Teresa's primary objective was to serve Jesus Christ who she believed was hidden in the faces of those who suffered. Jesus' words 'I thirst', when dying on the cross, were to become a kind of motto of the congregation. All along, she was adamant that the work could never become more important than Jesus Christ. To explain her reasons for undertaking the work, she would hold out her hand, splaying her fingers and thumb, and say, 'You did it to me,' recalling Jesus' words in the gospels that when you cared for the poor, the sick and the rejected, you were also caring for him.

Archbishop Perier sent the rule to Rome for approval, and in October 1950, the Vatican granted her permission to become a diocesan congregation for a three-year probationary period, pointing out that she would not be permitted to open a house outside the archdiocese of Calcutta until ten years had passed. Sister Teresa was now Mother Teresa, and no longer a maverick.

On the Feast of Our Lady of the Rosary the archbishop celebrated Mass in Creek Lane and the letter from Rome authorizing the order was read out by a delighted Father Van Exem. The Missionaries of Charity had now grown to seven, all former pupils of St Mary's. They had begun visiting families, taking people abandoned in the street to hospitals, providing medicine and running Sunday schools.

Because there were dozens of languages in India, Mother Teresa had decided to make English the language of the congregation. And she decided that as well as the traditional vows of poverty, chastity and obedience, her sisters would take a fourth vow, charity.

By now, each sister wore a simple white sari with blue trimmings, a long white veil, a crucifix pinned to her shoulder and a pair of sandals with no stockings. Their tightly structured daily timetable was similar to that of many religious orders of the period. They would rise at 4.40 a.m. and then, after Mass, prayer, breakfast and chores, would go out into the streets, praying their rosary as they walked, to help the poor in any way they could. They would return to the convent for lunch at 12.30 p.m., followed by spiritual reading, meditation and a period of adoration in the chapel. At 4.30 p.m. they would return to the streets, returning for supper at 7.30 p.m. After Evening Prayer in the chapel, they would retire to bed. Lights out and *magnum silencium* was at 9.45 p.m.

Mother Teresa, on the other hand, would often stay up till the early hours, crouched over her desk writing letters and, presumably, taking time to reflect on how the order, and in particular, each sister, was developing and whether or not she needed to address any specific issues. The congregation survived day to day, relying on begging or donations from benefactors. There were times when they didn't have enough food to go round or oil to cook with.

Newspapers and magazines in India began carrying stories about this odd but inspiring European nun in Calcutta. One consequence of this was that people, including nurses and doctors, offered to be volunteer helpers.

However, behind her outward confidence and zeal, Mother Teresa was struggling with doubts about God and her faith. Only her confessor,

Father Van Exem, and Archbishop Perier were aware of this. On 18 March 1953, she wrote to the archbishop about the 'terrible darkness within me', explaining that she had been experiencing these feelings ever since she had left the Loreto Sisters. If she thought they would disappear, she was wrong.

LOWER CIRCULAR ROAD

Following the expansion of the congregation, Michael Gomes had given Mother Teresa an extra floor in his house, but by the end of 1952, conditions had become unbearably cramped for her twenty-seven sisters. The sisters began praying that God would find them a larger home. Father Van Exem heard that a retired magistrate he knew was planning to leave his three-storey house on the busy Lower Circular Road, a short distance from Creek Lane, and move to Dhaka. After listening to the priest's enthusiastic description of the work the Missionaries of Charity were doing, the magistrate agreed to sell the house to them.

As Mother Teresa didn't have that sort of money, it was left to Archbishop Perier to

Mother Teresa during her prayers at the Missionary of the Pure Heart in Calcutta. Prayer was at the heart of Mother Teresa's work.

The first home
for the dying was
opened at the
Dakshineshwar
temple at Kali Ghat.

provide her with a loan. In February 1953, she and her sisters left Creek Lane, and the house on Lower Circular Road, became the congregation's mother house or headquarters.

Shortly after, the first four young women who had joined Sister Teresa at Creek Lane made their first vows, as Sister Agnes, Sister Gertrude, Sister Dorothy and Sister Margaret Mary, while Mother Teresa took her final vows as foundress.

Around this time, she wrote to Jacqueline de Decker, the Belgian social worker she had met at Patna, inviting her to become a spiritual member of the Missionaries of Charity and recruit others to do the same. She called de Decker her 'second self' and wanted each of her sisters also to have a second self. The young Belgian was delighted with this idea, and formed what later became the Sick and Suffering Co-Workers.

NIRMAL HRIDAY HOME FOR THE DYING

Mother Teresa had by now established a number of free schools but she decided that her first major project would be a home for those dying on the streets. She couldn't solve the problem, but at least she could provide care and love to some of those left abandoned.

When she raised the issue with a council health officer, he was impressed by her idea and took her across the city to the Kalighat district. When they reached the domes of the nineteenth-century Kali temple on the banks of a canal, he took her into an abandoned, long, single-storey whitewashed building, where pilgrims used to rest after worshipping Kali, the goddess of death and fertility. Looking around, Mother Teresa decided this was perfect and named it Nirmal Hriday (meaning 'pure heart' in Bengali) Home for Dying Destitutes.

She and her sisters began going into the streets to collect the dying, sometimes bringing them back in a wheelbarrow. Some of those brought in were suffering from malnutrition; others from disease. Later, people were brought in by ambulance. Mother Teresa had insisted that anyone must first of all be taken to the nearest hospital. If the hospital turned the person away, the home would then accept them. While conditions in Nirmal Hriday were primitive, at least those who died there did so in an atmosphere of care and compassion.

Making clear that she was not a social worker, Mother Teresa said of those taken into Nirmal Hriday, 'We help them to die with God. We help them to say sorry to God. To make peace with God according to their faith.'[4]

But the idea of Christians occupying a building next to one of the holiest Hindu places of worship was greeted with anger by some, who believed that they were really out to convert Hindus to Christianity. Things got ugly. Stones were thrown at the sisters and Mother Teresa even received a death threat. A city councillor demanded that the sisters leave Kali and move to another location.

After the police commissioner had visited the home, he reportedly told those who had complained, 'I have said that I will get rid of this foreign lady and I will do so, but you must first get your mothers and sisters to do what she is doing.'[5]

One evening, Mother Teresa noticed a crowd gathered in front of the temple. When she went outside, she saw that in the middle of the crowd

'It is Christ you tend in the poor. It is his wounds you bathe, his sores you clean, his limbs you bandage.'

lay a man on the pavement. Because it was thought he had cholera, no one dared touch him. Ignoring the crowd's warnings, Mother Teresa and her sisters picked him up and took him inside. The man turned out to be a priest from the Kali temple.

The care that the sisters showed to the priest, who died soon after, seems to have put a stop to the gossip that the Missionaries of Charity were engaged in covert conversions among Hindus. When someone remarked to Mother Teresa that she was lucky not to have been beaten or shot, she replied that she was ready to die for God.

In her book *Such a Vision of the Street*, Eileen Egan, an American humanitarian worker who had met Mother Teresa in Calcutta in the mid-1950s, recounts accompanying her to Sealdah railway station: 'In Sealdah, we picked our way over the prone bodies and possessions of the refugees, barely missing here the hand of a sleeping child, or there the belongings of an old woman crouching behind gunnysacks and staring out of sightless eyes. Among the massed brown bodies were men with chests like birdcages clad only in dhoti around their loins and women in rough cotton saris like the one worn by Mother Teresa, except that theirs were dun-coloured with dirt.'[6]

Describing those who came to her for help, Mother Teresa once told a priest, 'It is Christ you tend in the poor. It is his wounds you bathe, his sores you clean, his limbs you bandage. See beyond appearances, hear the words Jesus pronounced long ago; they are still operative today. "What you do to the least of mine you do to me." '[7]

Yet despite all of her work and the utter conviction with which she spoke to others about God, she was continuing to experience anxiety about what she described as a 'deep darkness and desolation' and a 'deep loneliness'.

An increasing number of volunteers, including some wealthy women from Calcutta society, were now coming forward to help. Mother Teresa was not only pricking consciences but, through her actions, also challenging the Hindu caste system that viewed some human beings as more or less worthless.

Someone who she especially inspired was Englishwoman Ann Blaikie, the wife of a lawyer working for British American Tobacco. Ann was part of the British ex-pat community and busied herself as a volunteer in a charity shop selling handicrafts and clothes. In 1954, after reading an article about Mother Teresa, she went to see her at a mother-and-baby clinic she ran and offered to provide toys for a children's Christmas party. Mother Teresa told her that what she really wanted was clothes for the children. Blaikie duly obliged. Mother Teresa then asked her if she could provide clothes for the Hindu children who would be attending her Diwali party and the Muslim children who would be attending her Ramadan party. Blaikie formed a small group of comfortably-off women to support the Missionaries of Charity's work. This group was to become the origins of the Co-Workers.

SHISHU BHAVAN CHILDREN'S HOME

Mother Teresa now started looking around for a property where she could care for orphans and other unwanted children. In doing this, she was rising to the challenge Pope Pius XII had issued in his 1946 encyclical

Quemadmodum ('Pleading for the Care of the World's Destitute Children').

Eventually in 1955, she found a two-storey house with a courtyard on Lower Circular Road close to her headquarters and called it Shishu Bhavan.

Soon police officers, social workers and others were bringing abandoned, sick and homeless babies and children to the sisters to look after. Some children were adopted by Indian families; others by families in Europe, Canada and the USA. Mother Teresa saw adoption as one of the ways of fighting abortion.

Initially, she accepted government grants for each child from the corporation, but later turned them down. The reason seems to be that she didn't want to get caught up in the rules and regulations that accompanied local authority funding.

Again, more volunteers came to help out, including Aruna Paul, a former Loreto pupil who had married businessman Swarat Paul, later Lord Paul. She used her connections with a textile factory to provide the sisters with new saris.

One of Mother Teresa's most influential supporters at this time was Dr B.C. Roy, chief minister of West Bengal and also a doctor whose patients had included Gandhi, Indian Prime Minister Jawaharlal Nehru and the king of Nepal. When he asked her if she would take charge of the four government-run vagrancy homes in Calcutta, she told him that

Mother Teresa had
little sense of God's
presence in her life.

she didn't have enough sisters to do the work. This might have been true. Alternatively, as with the children's grants she rejected, she might have refused the offer because of the bureaucracy she would have encountered in running the homes.

Her small band of sisters were finding themselves overwhelmed by the needs of the poor. Mother Teresa once said, 'In the choice of the works of the apostolate there was neither planning nor preconceived ideas. We started work as needs and opportunities arose. God showed what he wanted us to do.'[8]

THE ABSENCE OF GOD

Yet despite her tireless work for the poor and the sick and the hours she spent in prayer each day, she still had little sense of God's presence. The certainty and joy she had experienced following that defining moment on the train to Darjeeling had long deserted her. She was unable to see that this was not unusual, as the Bible showed. In fact, she was experiencing the same kind of emptiness depicted in some of the psalms and in the book of Job. When Jesus told the father of a child with epilepsy that everything was possible to those with faith, he replied, 'I have faith. Help my lack of faith.' And Jesus himself had suffered the anguish of feeling God's absence both in the Garden of Gethsemane and on the cross.

In February 1956, she wrote to Archbishop Perier of 'that terrible emptiness, that feeling of absence of God'. He replied by pointing out that this absence of God was common in the mystical life. It was God's way of leading her to a deeper trust in him and not in the things of the world.

This still didn't console her. Soon after, she joined her novices on a retreat led by Father Lawrence Picachy, Rector of St Xavier's, a Jesuit college in the city. She also decided to open up to him about the spiritual darkness she was going through, and he eventually became her new confessor.

Her letters to Archbishop Perier continued. The following year, she told him that despite her deep longing for God, she felt unwanted by God, that she had no faith, no love, no zeal, and that heaven meant nothing to her. She had resolved to mask her trials by smiling and maintaining her natural cheerfulness.

As she was the superior of the congregation, there was no way she could reveal what she was going through to her sisters. Instead she continued to go about her work in her usual cheerful way.

LEPROSY

One of the most widespread diseases in Calcutta was leprosy. The city had a leper population of an estimated 30,000, many living in poor districts. The terrible disease provoked fear amongst many, leading to lepers being shunned.

For Mother Teresa, leprosy had a significance that other diseases didn't. The gospels contain several stories of Jesus curing lepers. She may have also had in her mind the story of Father Damien De Veuster, a Belgian missionary who worked with the lepers in Hawaii in the nineteenth century.

The trigger for her mission to the city's lepers seems to have been an incident when five lepers who had been thrown out of their homes came to her for help. This, and the closure of the city's only specialist hospital for lepers, despite her campaign to keep it open, galvanized her into action.

She once remarked of lepers, 'They live by begging, since no one will employ them. On Sundays they slip into Calcutta and beg around Christian churches. On Friday evenings they work Muslim mosques. Of course they are also around Hindu temples. But they don't remain long at these places. When begging is no good, they move back into their various enclaves in the slums.'[9]

Some of her sisters were understandably worried about contracting the disease. After all, Father Damien had done just that, dying from the same disease as that of the people he had served. Mother Teresa's response was to trust in God.

In 1957, she launched her first mobile clinic when Catholic Relief Services in the US paid for a van to be converted into a mobile dispensary. A doctor she knew agreed to act as the driver, and the dispensary visited the districts of Howrah, Tilajala, Dhappa and Moti Jihil, carrying medicines, food and powdered milk.

Ann Blaikie and her team agreed to take over fundraising for her leprosy work. Small groups of women met to roll bandages and to make paper bags for the lepers' pills, while others went out into the streets with tins marked 'Touch the leper with your kindness'.

A ray of light finally pierced Mother Teresa's spiritual darkness in 1958 during a requiem Mass for Pope Pius XII in Our Lady of the Rosary Cathedral. 'Today my soul is filled with love, with joy untold,' she wrote. Nevertheless, it turned out to be a brief respite.

In July 1959 she wrote a detailed account of her unbearable spiritual

Seriously and terminally ill patients lie on beds at Nirmal Hriday.

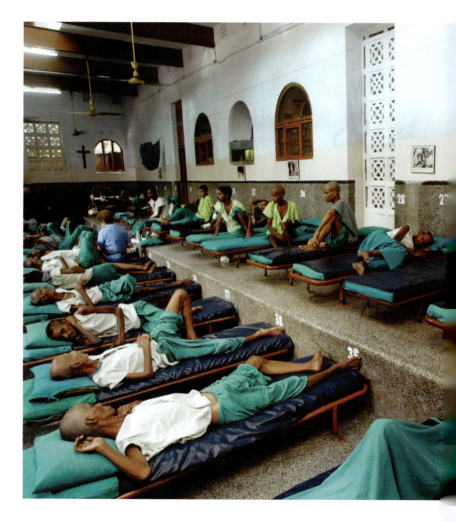

emptiness to Father Picachy: 'The darkness is so dark – and I am alone – Unwanted, forsaken. – The loneliness of the heart that wants love is unbearable. – Where is my faith? – even deep down, right in, there is nothing but emptiness & darkness – My God – how painful is this unknown pain. It pains without ceasing. – I have no faith – I dare not utter the words & thoughts that crowd in my heart... So many unanswered questions live within me – I am afraid to uncover them – because of the blasphemy – If there be a God – please forgive me... Love – the word – it brings nothing. – I am told God loves me – and yet the reality of darkness & coldness & emptiness is so great that nothing touches my soul.'[10]

Yet, despite all of these feelings and questions, she was unswerving in her trust in God, promising to accept all of this. She would not go back on that secret vow she made in 1942 to refuse Jesus nothing.

Mother Teresa was already planning to open other houses in India. Technically, as a diocesan congregation, the Missionaries of Charity had to wait ten years before they could do this. The Calcutta newspaper *The Statesman* had carried stories about her, and a number of bishops had invited her to come and work in their dioceses. In 1959, a group of Missionaries of Charity set up a house in the city of Ranchi, north-west of Calcutta. This was soon followed by houses in Delhi, Jhansi and Agra.

In just ten years, Mother Teresa's congregation had grown to eighty-five sisters. It had set up free schools, leprosy clinics, mother-and-baby clinics, a home for the dying, and a children's home. In addition, the sisters provided food and clothing to the queues of men and women who turned up at the mother house and other centres. And she had now spread out from Calcutta to other parts of India. It was a remarkable achievement, especially considering that she began with no money or help and that she had to overcome opposition from her own Loreto Sisters and also those who thought she was only out to convert Hindus to Christianity.

It was even more remarkable that all of this was achieved while feeling very little presence whatsoever of God in her life.

The publicity that she had attracted during these ten years had spread beyond India to other countries, including Germany and the US. And Catholics in the world's richest country were not satisfied reading about her – they wanted to meet her.

Chapter 4
A NUN ON A MISSION

Mother Teresa arrived in Las Vegas in October 1960 at the same time as Frank Sinatra was in concert at the Sands Hotel. She would probably have been as unfamiliar with the American superstar as she was with the rows of glitzy casinos and nightclubs that lined the Strip. If you are talking about a culture shock, they don't get much bigger than this. Novelist Chuck Palahniuk had once remarked of the city, 'Las Vegas looks the way you'd imagine heaven must look at night.'[1] Mother Teresa had a different idea of heaven.

This was her first trip overseas since entering religious life in 1928 and her first visit to America. It had been organized by Catholic Relief Services, who had provided funding for her mobile dispensary. She had been invited to address the National Council of Catholic Women, whose programme 'The Works of Peace' provided money for women's health and development projects around the world.

Because she had never spoken in public before, she initially turned down the invitation and instead proposed Eileen Egan, who had got to know her work well since first meeting her in the mid-1950s. Archbishop Perier, however, told her that she should go herself. He must have realized what a powerful witness to faith she would be.

Mother Teresa knew little about Western society. To keep the attention of her sisters focused on God and their mission to the poor, she didn't allow radios, televisions or newspapers in her houses. During her six weeks in Dublin in 1928, she seems never to have ventured beyond the convent gates.

After being welcomed by the organizers, including Cardinal Richard Cushing, Archbishop of Boston (who nicknamed her 'Mahatma

Gandhi'), she must have wondered as she stepped onto the podium how she would even begin to make a connection between the squalid lives of those she worked with in the slums of Calcutta and the 3,000 smartly dressed Catholics sitting in front of her. She began by joining the palms of her hands together and then bowing her head, explaining that this was the traditional way to greet someone in India. She then did the only thing she could do: she spoke from her heart, telling the audience how she and her 119 sisters, all but three of them Indian, were trying to bring the love of Jesus Christ to the poor, the rejected, the sick and the dying. She may have lacked the skills of someone more used to public speaking but this did not matter, judging by the applause that rang around the hall when she had finished her address.

After her speech, she sat in a booth in the exhibit hall answering questions about herself and her work in Calcutta from the dozens of women who crowded around her. A number of them slipped money into the canvas bag she carried with her everywhere.

Yet behind her talk of God's love and of finding Christ in the poor, she was still battling with doubts about her faith. Only a few days before flying to the US, she had written to Father Picachy about her longing for God and the accompanying feeling of darkness, loneliness and aloneness: 'Heaven from every side is closed.'[2] Was God real? Did she believe? What was the point of her work? These and many other questions were constantly swirling around in her head.

After Las Vegas, she gave a talk in a packed high school in the small farming town of Henry in Illinois. She had gone there because local parishes had been sending funds for the mother-and-baby clinics she ran. Then she visited Chicago and Washington, DC, where she met Cardinal Patrick O'Boyle, before travelling to New York. By coincidence, she found herself staying in the same religious house as Mother Anna Dengel, who had provided her with her medical training in Patna. The two of them swapped stories, and Mother Dengel explained that her order had now expanded to Pakistan, Africa and Latin America, and she had also opened a midwifery institute in New Mexico to train midwives.

In New York, Mother Teresa also met another remarkable woman – journalist and activist Dorothy Day. Day had converted to Catholicism in 1927 at the age of thirty, after turning her back on socialism and a Bohemian lifestyle in Greenwich Village that had led her to have an abortion in an attempt to prevent a lover from leaving her – a decision she was to regret for the rest of her life. She had founded the *Catholic Worker* newspaper and set up a string of houses for the poor across America.

Day gave Mother Teresa her first real introduction to the underbelly of Western society when she took her on a tour of New York's Lower East Side, known for its cheap hotels. Mother Teresa was shocked at the number of dishevelled men she came across lying on the pavement.

Before returning to Calcutta, she stopped off in London, where she met an Oxfam representative, who promised to get some anti-leprosy drugs sent to her through ICI. She then flew on to West Germany to visit the offices of Misereor, a Catholic aid agency, which had featured her in its magazine. The director told her it would fund the construction of a home for the dying in Delhi, as long as she was able to provide detailed accounts. Mother Teresa replied that her sisters didn't have time for that, but assured him that any money she received would go to the home. It was agreed that Misereor would provide an estimate of the building costs and its accountants would provide a financial report.

While in Germany, she also visited the concentration camp in Dachau, walking around it in silence, fingering her rosary. As she left, all she could say was, 'To think that human beings could do these things to other human beings.'[3]

After a brief stop in Geneva, where she addressed the representatives of international Catholic organizations, she arrived in Rome and went to see Cardinal Agagianian and Archbishop Pietro Sigismondi at the Sacred Congregation for the Propagation of the Faith to ask that the Missionaries of Charity become an institute established by pontifical right. This would remove the Missionaries of Charity from the authority of local bishops and allow it to expand overseas, something Mother Teresa was impatient to do, and probably more so now having heard from Mother Dengel about the growth of the Medical Mission Sisters. She presented them with a brief document and answered their questions about their work and funding.

When the Missionaries of Charity gathered together for their first general chapter the following year, unsurprisingly, Mother Teresa was elected superior general.

Word about her continued to spread both in India and abroad, and in 1962, she received two prestigious awards. The Indian government presented her with the Padmashree Award for her contribution to social work (she placed the medal around the statue of the Virgin Mary in Nirmal Hriday). And in a ceremony in Manila, in the Philippines, she received the Ramon Magsaysay Award for International Understanding.

During the 1960s
Mother Teresa
responded to many
invitations to travel
outside India and
talk about the work
in Calcutta.

DARKNESS

But neither the praise heaped on her in America nor these accolades were enough to take away the spiritual emptiness she still felt. She decided to confess her spiritual struggles to another Jesuit, Father Joseph Neuner, an Austrian theologian who lectured at Morning Star College in Calcutta. She wrote to him that: 'The place of God in my soul is blank. – There is no God in me. – When the pain and longing is so great – I just long & long for God – and then it is that I feel – He does not want me – He is not there.'[4]

Yet again she ended in a note of complete trust, or what some may prefer to call blind faith, emphasizing that she considered herself insignificant in God's greater scheme of things and saying, 'I am perfectly happy – to be God's flower of the field,'[5] a phrase that evoked St Thérèse of Lisieux, popularly known as 'The Little Flower'.

Father Neuner responded by reassuring her that her lack of feeling God's presence in her life was not a failure on her part. She was simply going through the dark night of the soul. St Thérèse of Lisieux had experienced similar feelings, leading her to say in the midst of her doubts, 'I choose to believe.' Mother Teresa's longing for God was, he reassured her, proof that God was present in the middle of her darkness.

Although Archbishop Perier had told her much the same, it was Father Neuner who provided Mother Teresa with the consolation she had been seeking. She replied, 'For the first time in these eleven years – I have come to love the darkness.'[6] She could now see it as a sharing of the pain and darkness Jesus himself experienced. She would surrender herself to him. She told Father Neuner that the advice he had given her 'will carry me for a long time'. She later said, 'If I ever become a saint – I will surely be one of darkness.'[7]

THE MISSIONARY BROTHERS OF CHARITY

The Missionaries of Charity now numbered nearly 200 sisters, but Mother Teresa decided that she needed a congregation of brothers to help her, thinking that men would be suited better than women to some aspects of the work. Her first recruits were three young Bengali men, who moved into the Shishu Bhavan children's home. The idea was that they would live the same life as the sisters and undertake work with the poor.

Although many male orders – Franciscans, Dominicans, Carmelites, Benedictines – had given birth to female branches, it was not so common for a female order to produce a male offshoot. Mother Teresa was aware that Rome didn't permit a woman to be head of a male congregation.

Because of this, she needed to find a priest with the right kind of vision, energy and holiness to lead the brothers. The solution to her problem turned out to be a tall, bearded thirty-year-old Australian Jesuit, Father Ian Travers-Ball. Father Ian – a former insurance salesman who had overcome an addiction to gambling – had heard Mother Teresa give a talk to a group of seminarians at Poona in 1962 and, soon after, he had spent a month working with the Missionaries of Charity as part of his training. This experience confirmed in him a desire to work with the poor.

Father Pedro Arrupe, head of the Jesuits at the time, granted him three years' absence from the order, after which he could renew his commitment for a further three years with the brothers or return to the Jesuits.

In 1966, Father Ian left the Jesuits and took charge of the brothers. He proved to be an inspired choice by Mother Teresa. Initially, the brothers had simply supported the work of the sisters. In the home for the dying they cared for the men, while the sisters cared for the women. If the sisters came across boys and men in need of care, they would send them to the brothers. Having greater physical strength, the brothers were invaluable when it came to lifting patients or carrying heavy loads.

But while Mother Teresa and Father Ian shared the same vision of serving Jesus Christ through caring for the poorest of the poor, they didn't always see eye to eye.

The Second Vatican Council, convened by Pius XII's successor, Pope John XXIII, had begun to introduce major changes to religious life in order to help it adapt and respond to the modern world. Many religious orders were beginning to abandon the traditional habit and leave their convents, priories and friaries for small houses. Father Ian was perhaps more tuned into these new ways of thinking than Mother Teresa. He had contributed to a number of theological journals, including *The Month, America* and *Review for Religious*. He had also written for the Catholic Enquiry Centre in Poona and set up a monthly magazine.

A seemingly trivial incident over sleeping arrangements divided Mother Teresa and Father Ian. Some of the brothers had vacated the dormitory at Shishu Bhavan for the terrace. When Mother Teresa heard about this, she informed Father Ian that the brothers must sleep in the dormitory. He told her that it was not for her to tell them where they were to sleep. Soon after, they had another disagreement when Father Ian replaced some iron beds with roll-up mattresses to make more room in what had become a very crowded house. She told him that sleeping on the damp floor would not be good for the brothers' health. Father Ian disagreed, having a more flexible approach to religious life than she did. He was determined to run the congregation his way, believing they were not simply an extension of the sisters, but a community in their own right.

Father Ian later wrote: 'I must say that she gave me total freedom, even when she disagreed with me. But it has to be said that she could be annoyed and piqued – and show it. On such points, I could have given way, and she would have been very happy to have her way. Where I held my ground she accepted – always graciously in the end, I must add. She was wonderful in not taking offence.'[8]

Needing more space, the brothers moved out of Shishu Bhavan and into rented accommodation, eventually moving into a property in the docks. Father Ian also revised the congregation's constitution, feeling that the original one devised by Mother Teresa was no longer adequate. In 1967, the Vatican approved them as a diocesan congregation, and the following year Father Ian changed his name to Brother Andrew.

A CHANGING CHURCH

Following the death of Pope John XXIII of stomach cancer in June 1963, Cardinal Giovanni Battista Montini had been elected his successor, taking the name Paul VI. He had the task of helping the Catholic Church adapt to the new ways of thinking about faith that had come out of the Second Vatican Council. One of the key issues for the bishops gathered in Rome was how the church related to those of other religions. In the past, Catholic

teaching had insisted that there was no salvation outside the Catholic Church. That had become a difficult theological position to hold in the 1960s when television, radio and emigration had broken down some of the barriers that had largely kept Catholics apart from other religious traditions. If there was no salvation outside the Catholic Church, then the vast majority of people on the planet could have no expectation of a life with God beyond death.

This had never been Mother Teresa's view of those men and women in Nirmal Hriday who she believed were going home to God. She had shown the church how Catholics could live with and relate to those of other faiths without in any way compromising their own beliefs. She provided care to Hindus, Muslims, Sikhs, Buddhists, Jains – anyone – and, because of this, she drew support from all sections of Calcutta society. While the bishops in Rome debated what interfaith dialogue meant, for her it was not about doctrine or the finer points of theology, but about people. For Mother Teresa,

Pope Paul VI walking towards the altar at the 38th International Eucharistic Congress in Bombay, 3 December 1964. Pope Paul VI's visit to India was important for its Catholic minority.

it was quite simple: each person was made in the image and likeness of God, and God loved each person.

In December 1964, Bombay hosted the International Eucharistic Congress, a gathering of Catholics from around the world, and Pope Paul VI arrived to open it. Earlier that year, he had made a pilgrimage to Israel and Jordan, becoming the first pope to set foot in the Holy Land since Peter. He would now become the first pope to visit India. For India's Catholics, a minority community, the visit was of enormous importance. It showed them that they were not forgotten and underlined that they were part of a global religion.

At the close of the congress, Pope Paul VI donated the white Lincoln convertible car given to him by some American Catholics to the Missionaries of Charity. Mother Teresa decided to raffle it. The money it raised went towards creating Shanti Nagar ('the Place of Peace'), a leper village built on land donated by the Indian government. Her idea was to help lepers become self-sufficient and not have to cope with rejection. They lived in cottages, learned building skills, how to grow rice, look after cattle, make baskets and run a printing press.

Both the Missionaries of Charity's work and Mother Teresa's reputation continued to grow. Mother Teresa was now beginning to travel around India more frequently, looking for needs that her sisters could meet. The train from Calcutta to Delhi passed through a station called Eck Dil ('one heart') and another called Prempur ('full of love'). Mother Teresa was fond of telling her sisters that if they put the two names together they would have a perfect community. When the Indian prime minister, Jawaharlal Nehru, came to open a children's home in Delhi,

One of the patients at
Nirmal Hriday home
gets the attention of
Mother Teresa.

Mother Teresa asked him if he wanted her to explain what the Missionaries of Charity did. 'No, Mother, you need not tell me about your work. I know about it. That is why I have come,' he replied.[9]

In 1965, the Vatican finally granted the Missionaries of Charity the status of an institute of pontifical right. Mother Teresa decided to open the first house outside India in Venezuela. During the sessions of the Second Vatican Council, Bishop Benitez Naerquisimeto of Venezuela had told Archbishop Robert Knox, the papal internuncio to New Delhi, that he was concerned that the church was failing to help many of the poor in his diocese. When Archbishop Knox told him about Mother Teresa, he decided to invite her to send some of her sisters to open a house.

In July 1965, a group of sisters under the leadership of Sister Nirmala, a former Hindu who had been one of Mother Teresa's first sisters, landed at Caracas Airport. Later that day, they arrived in Cocorte, a small town in the north of the country, and moved into the abandoned rectory of the Church of San Jeronimo. They began visiting poor families, setting up classes in sewing, typing and basic English. They also taught the catechism and helped prepare young people for their first Holy Communion. In turn, the sisters learned Spanish from the local women, and they were also taught how to drive the station wagon that had been given to them.

Pope Paul VI was so impressed by the work that she was doing that he invited Mother Teresa to open a house in Rome. She must have been surprised by this invitation, as there were already dozens of female congregations working across the city. In August 1968, she arrived with a group of sisters in the parish of Santo Stefano and, after a brief stay in a small house in the suburbs, moved into a property in Tor Fiscale, establishing a day-care centre for children, and running sewing classes for girls, and literacy classes. Later that year, Mother Teresa opened her first house in Africa, in Tanzania. The Missionaries of Charity congregation was finally becoming truly international.

MUGGERIDGE

The media interest in Mother Teresa continued and in 1968 she was interviewed for a BBC television programme by Malcolm Muggeridge, an English journalist and writer who was on a personal spiritual search. By all accounts, the interview, done at the Holy Child Convent in central London, wasn't particularly remarkable. Mother Teresa simply explained what she and her sisters did and why they did it, just as she had done when she addressed the National Council of Catholic Women in Las Vegas.

When the thirty-minute programme was broadcast late at night, it produced an extraordinary reaction from the public, with many writing to the BBC to say how moved they had been by what she had said. Some even enclosed cheques or postal orders.

The following year, Muggeridge and a television crew flew to Calcutta to make *Something Beautiful for God*, a documentary about Mother Teresa.

Muggeridge had lived in Calcutta for a while in the 1930s when he worked on *The Statesman* newspaper. But the Calcutta he had known was one of servants, drinks parties and canters around the Jodhpur Club. He knew little about the countless destitute men and women who lay dying in the city's streets.

What he witnessed at the Nirmal Hriday home for the dying was to have a profound impact on him. It wasn't just the love that Mother Teresa and her sisters gave to those they scooped up off the streets. Muggeridge believed a miracle had taken place during the filming. Cameraman Ken Macmillan, whose work included the ground-breaking Kenneth Clark series *Civilisation*, had told Muggeridge that the light in the home for the dying wasn't good for filming. Muggeridge later wrote in his book *Something Beautiful for God*, 'We had only one small light with us, and to get the place adequately lit in the time at our disposal was quite impossible. It was decided that, nonetheless, Ken should have a go, but by way of insurance he took, as well, some film in an outside courtyard where some of the inmates were sitting in the sun. In the processed film, the part taken inside was bathed in a particularly beautiful soft light, whereas the part taken outside was rather dim and confused.'[10]

Macmillan was unable to explain this odd result. Technically, it was impossible, he said. Muggeridge, however, believed that the light inside the home was the result of supernatural intervention. When he showed the film to a group of bishops and priests at the Catholic Radio and Television Centre at Hatch End, near London, he expected them to share his wonder at this divine intervention. Not so. They suggested that the results were more likely due to the adjustment of the camera or the quality of the film stock.

Muggeridge was taken aback by what he seemed to see as a lack of faith in God's ability to work miracles.

Mother Teresa had never been keen on publicity, but she recognized that the right kind could serve God. As a result of the Muggeridge film, she was now on her way to becoming a household name.

When the president of India, Shri Varahagiri Venkata Giri, presented her with the Nehru Award in 1969, he said she had 'transcended all barriers of race, religion, creed and nation. In this troubled world of today, embittered by numerous conflicts and hatred, the life and work of Mother Teresa brings new hope for the future of mankind.'[11]

In *Mother Teresa: Beyond the Image*, Anne Sebba suggested that the awards and cheques given to Mother Teresa reflected something of the age. 'It was, after all, the 1960s and there was a potent sense of idealism around, which she harnessed better than anyone else. There was a distinct feeling that here was someone who was actually doing something to right the ills of the world instead of merely demonstrating, or smoking dope, while talking of doing something.'[12]

There was something in that. Every age needs its heroes and heroines. Mother Teresa's counter-cultural lifestyle, her compassion for the poor and the weak, her rejection of consumerism, and her identification with India, seen by many in the West at that time as a third-world country, had turned her into the ideal heroine for a Western society in search of meaning and ideals. However, she never saw herself in such a light. She was simply an instrument of God. But there was little she could do to stop this adulation. And it was only to become even greater.

Chapter 5
THE LIVING SAINT

Sandwiched between the Hudson River and East River and connected to Manhattan by the six-lane Washington Bridge, the Bronx had once been a prosperous district of New York – but by 1971 it had collapsed into a ghetto. Many of its tenements and abandoned burned-out buildings had become havens to street gangs, muggers and drug addicts. Crime against the elderly was so bad that the New York Police Department had set up special teams of officers to patrol the streets. While once the majority of the population had been Italian or Jewish, they were now mostly either black or Puerto Ricans mostly living in crowded and poor conditions.

When Cardinal Terence Cooke, the archbishop of New York, invited Mother Teresa to open a house in the South Bronx, she had no hesitation in accepting the challenge. This was exactly the kind of area she wanted to send her sisters to.

Walking with Dorothy Day through the streets of New York's East Side had given her a glimpse of the poverty and lack of hope that lurked under the sheen of affluent Western cities. She once said, 'Each time I go to Europe and America I am struck by the unhappiness of so many people living in those rich countries; so many broken homes, children not looked after by their parents. Their first duty is to work among their own people, bringing together separated couples, building good homes where the children receive their parents' love. They have material wealth; they lack spiritual values.'[1]

Asked once by a priest how she thought she could serve the poor in New York, she replied, 'We can be a bridge between those who have and those who have less.'[2] It was a typical Mother Teresa response. She didn't believe in devising detailed plans or targets for the sisters when they began a new mission, but preferred to let events and God take their course. She once said,

'I don't want the work to become a business but to remain a work of love' and another time, 'Pay no attention to numbers; what matters is the people.'[3]

In 1971, five sisters arrived at JFK Airport, each carrying their own cooking utensils along with a rolled-up mattress. Initially, they lived with the Handmaids of Mary in a convent in Harlem before moving into a three-storey red-brick house in the heart of the South Bronx.

Given the large Hispanic population, one of the first things the sisters did was to enrol in Spanish classes at a Catholic high school. Gradually they got to know the families in the neighbourhood and were soon accompanying them on the subway to court hearings and on their visits to see prisoners on Rikers Island. They became a familiar sight, visiting both the elderly, doing their washing and cleaning and praying with them, and the sick in hospitals and nursing homes.

When Mother Teresa arrived in New York in October 1971, she had two appointments. Most importantly, she wanted to see how the sisters were adapting to their new mission and to give them advice and support. But she had also been informed that she was one of eight outstanding individuals to receive an award for her humanitarian work from the Joseph P. Kennedy Jr. Foundation.

At the ceremony at the John F. Kennedy Center for the Performing Arts in Washington, DC, a clip from *Something Beautiful for God* was shown before she came up onto the stage to receive her award and a cheque for $12,000 from the smiling Senator Kennedy. The money enabled her to refurbish a home for the mentally and physically disabled near Calcutta airport.

While in the US, Mother Teresa met up with Malcolm Muggeridge and the two of them embarked on a round of press and television interviews to

'Children, ask your parents to teach you how to pray. That is the beginning.'

promote the book *Something Beautiful for God*. They were guests on both the David Frost and Barbara Walters shows, two of the most popular in America. When she was challenged about how little her sisters could help given that there were so many needs, she replied, 'I do not add up. I only subtract from the total number of poor or dying. With children, one dollar saves a life. Could you say one dollar buys a life? No, but it is used to save it.'[4] During one of the interviews, an advert for slimming products appeared on the monitor in front of her, leading her to remark, 'And I spend all my time trying to put an ounce of flesh on bare bones.'

She flew from New York to Toronto to share a platform at a conference with Jean Vanier. Like Mother Teresa, he had also responded in a radical way to the needs of the disadvantaged. He had quit his teaching post at the University of Toronto and decided to commit his life to setting up houses for those with learning disabilities. His aim was to create a family atmosphere, far removed from the impersonal conditions that were the hallmarks of the large institutions. His first house in France was called L'Arche (French for 'Ark'), and the name was adopted for the other houses that soon began to spring up.

The theme of the conference in Toronto was 'Secret of Peace', and the city's Massey Hall was packed, mainly with students and other young people, eager to learn how they could make a difference in the world. Mother Teresa told them that before they went on peace demonstrations they should be at peace with those people they knew. She urged them to respond to the needs of the poor and suffering in their own cities and towns, what she called 'little Calcuttas'. Good works alone were not enough, she went on, telling them, 'Children, ask your parents to teach you how to pray. That is the beginning.'[5]

UNDER FIRE

According to Anne Sebba in her book *Mother Teresa: Beyond the Image*, in 1972 Mother Teresa bumped into Australian-born writer and feminist Germaine Greer on a plane. Her book *The Female Eunuch*, published two years before, had become a best-seller. Speaking about it to *The New York Times*, Greer said, 'Women have somehow been separated from their libido, from their faculty of desire, from their sexuality. They've become suspicious about it. Like beasts, for example, who are castrated in farming in order to serve their master's ulterior motives – to be fattened or made docile – women have been cut off from their capacity for action.'[6]

Greer had been particularly scathing about Mother Teresa's intervention in Bangladesh following its declaration of independence in 1971 after a bitter civil war. One consequence of the fighting was the rape of countless girls and women by Pakistani soldiers. Some estimates put the number at 200,000. Those women who became pregnant received no help from their families. Instead, in accordance with Islam, they were rejected. Mother Teresa responded by setting up several houses to care for the victims. She also taught them how to support themselves financially by selling puffed rice in Dakha market.

'When she went to Dakha two days after its liberation from the Pakistanis in 1972, 3,000 named women had been found in the army bunkers,' said Greer. 'Their saris had been taken away so that they would not hang themselves. The pregnant ones needed abortions. Mother Teresa offered them no option but to bear the offspring of hate. There is no room in Mother Teresa's universe for the moral priorities of others.

*Mother Teresa's
unwavering views on
abortion were to attract
publicity and provoke
controversy many times
throughout her life.*

There is no question of offering suffering women a chance.'[7]

Greer went on to claim that some aid workers had told her that some women with complications of late pregnancy, or who were miscarrying, had arrived at clinics run by the Missionaries of Charity only to be turned away. Was she correct? We don't know. What we do know is that she saw Mother Teresa as someone who put back the clock where the role of women was concerned. According to Greer, she was docile, unquestioning of patriarchal authority and an advocate of a view of sexuality that kept women imprisoned.

Mother Teresa's unwavering views on abortion were to attract publicity and provoke controversy many times throughout her life.

FAILURES

In 1972, convinced that love and forgiveness were the answer to violence and war, Mother Teresa landed in Belfast with four sisters. Northern Ireland had become a battleground between paramilitaries who were divided along Catholic–Protestant lines, even though the violence was about land and who governed it. The British government's decision to send in troops had not brought peace to the streets but had only exacerbated the situation. To the IRA, they were a force of occupation. When a civil rights march in the Bogside district of Derry turned into a riot, British soldiers had opened fire, killing thirteen and injuring seventeen.

Mother Teresa must have hoped that those behind the sectarian violence and bombings that were tearing Northern Ireland apart could also come round to her viewpoint. After all, both sides in the conflict claimed to be Christian.

Mother Teresa praying during the dedication ceremony at her 400th worldwide mission, in Tijuana, Mexico, 1 July 1988. The Tijuana mission provides shelter for the homeless, the terminally ill and unwed mothers.

The Missionaries of Charity were no strangers to urban warfare. Two years before, a group of sisters had set up a house in Amman, in Jordan, and then found themselves caught up in a ten-day civil war between the Jordanian Army and the Palestinian Liberation Organization. Because of the bombings and gunfire, they were forced to sleep in the corridor of the house.

Mother Teresa and her sisters moved into a derelict council house in the Catholic area of Ballymurphy. The curate who had previously lived there had been shot dead – giving an indication of how dangerous the city had become. Mother Teresa's plan was for the Missionaries of Charity to work with some Anglican sisters as a symbol of Christian unity.

However, the sisters were not greeted enthusiastically by everyone, it seems, and it wasn't long before they packed their bags and left. Why this happened has never been clear. Perhaps Mother Teresa had failed to understand properly the complex political and religious history that lay behind the violence.

Things didn't go to plan for her either in Sri Lanka when she was forced to abandon her mission in Colombo after the government expelled all foreign religious orders.

SUSTAINED BY PRAYER

Despite Greer's stinging criticism and the failures in Northern Ireland and Sri Lanka, Mother Teresa's reputation was undiminished. The following year, at a ceremony in London, she became the first recipient of the Templeton Prize for Progress in Religion.

Prayer was the bedrock upon which she and her sisters based their work (she often gave out prayer cards to those whom she met, referring to them as her 'business cards'). Despite experiencing a blank most of the time she prayed, she persevered each day of her life. 'If you are searching for God and do not know where to begin,' she once explained, 'learn to pray and take the trouble to pray every day. You can pray any time, anywhere. You do not have to be in a chapel or a church. You can pray at work – work doesn't have to stop prayer and prayer doesn't have to stop work.'[8]

So, she asked that each of her houses be twinned with a contemplative convent. To have contemplatives praying for the congregation would strengthen their work, she believed. Within a year, around 400 convents and monasteries had signed up.

In 1976, when she attended the International Eucharistic Congress in Philadelphia, she announced that she was starting a new branch of the Missionaries of Charity, the Contemplative Missionaries of Charity. Sister Nirmala, who had headed up the community in Venezuela, was put in charge of the first house, along Union Avenue in the Bronx. The sisters were not to be entirely enclosed, like orders such as the Poor Clares. Instead they visited the isolated and the sick in hospital and invited locals to pray with them.

Explaining her choice of location for the new initiative, Mother Teresa later said, 'We all must take the time to be silent and to contemplate, especially those who live in big cities like London and New York, where everything moves so fast. This is why I decided to open our first home for contemplative sisters (whose vocation is to pray most of the day) in New York instead of the Himalayas, because I felt silence and contemplation were needed more in the cities of the world.'[9]

Three years later, she founded a congregation of contemplative brothers.

THE ROLE OF WOMEN

In 1975, realizing that she was someone who made it onto the front pages when she spoke about issues, the Vatican sent her as part of their official delegation to the UN's International Women's Conference in Mexico City (earlier that year, the UN's Food and Agriculture Organization had recognized her humanitarian works by striking a medal bearing her image).

The main focus of the conference was to discuss full equality for women, an end to discrimination and the promotion of their rights – the same kinds of things that Germaine Greer was arguing for.

When Mother Teresa told delegates that the vocation of women was to make a happy home for their husbands and children, it's reasonable to assume that some in the audience would have been shocked and outraged.

And it was clear she did not speak for all Catholic women, even for those in religious orders. Many had rejected Pope Paul VI's 1968 encyclical *Humanae Vitae* ('Of Human Life'), which forbade the use of artificial contraception, seeing it as unrealistic and evidence that the church had little understanding of contemporary women. Mother Teresa, on the other hand, had no problem with the encyclical. She believed the purpose of sex was to bring about children. Her idea of feminism (not that she would ever have used the word) was about living a life of love, compassion, sacrifice and service, not engaging in a battle to usurp power from men and trying to do away with the differences between the sexes.

When she returned to Calcutta, Father Edward Le Joly, one of her spiritual directors, asked her, 'How was Mexico, Mother?'

'Too much politics,' she replied. 'Disappointing. They did not mention God.'[10]

LIBERATION THEOLOGY

Elsewhere in Latin America, Marxism was being mixed with Catholicism to produce a powerful cocktail. Sparked by Vatican II's call for the Catholic Church to identify with the poor, what became known as liberation theology had developed as a reaction to the widespread poverty of the continent and the injustice caused by political, economic and social systems. It borrowed ideas about class struggle from Marxism and saw Jesus not just as a religious figure but also someone who had a political message. At the second general conference of Latin American bishops (CELAM), in Medellin, Colombia, in 1968, support was given to theologians such as Peruvian Gustavo Gutierrez, who argued that this was the way to transform society and bring about the kingdom of God. To some extent, he could be seen to be echoing Pope Paul VI's encyclical *Populorum Progressio* ('The Development of Peoples') in which the Pope had warned that in the long run the North South divide would be much more dangerous to the world than the East West conflict.

Rickshaws pass the long daily food queue outside the mother house in Calcutta.

Ever since leaving behind the Sisters of Loreto in 1948 and beginning a new life in the Calcutta slums, Mother Teresa had made what she called the poorest of the poor her priority. She once said, 'To know the problem of poverty intellectually is not to understand it. It is not by reading, talking, walking in the slums...that we come to understand it and to discover what it has of bad and good. We have to dive into it, live it, share it.'[11]

Given that the slogan of liberation theology was 'the preferential option for the poor', she would have seemed a natural supporter. She wasn't. The model of the Catholic Church adopted by theologians like Gutierrez was not the traditional hierarchical pyramid of the Pope at the top, bishops and clergy in the middle and the people at the bottom, the one Mother Teresa subscribed to. Instead the church was formed from what became known as basic Christian communities, where very often lay people or religious sisters were the leaders, not just priests.

While the Missionaries of Charity might not have embraced liberation theology and basic Christian communities, they were very active in grassroots Catholicism in Latin America. In Peru, for example, because of the shortage of priests, her sisters took on all the duties of a priest, with the exception of celebrating Mass and hearing confession.

'In practice they are like deacons,' Mother Teresa explained. 'Take the case of marriages: the sisters make all the preparatory arrangements and have the marriages celebrated. In one place, they had thirty marriages celebrated together. In another village, they regularized the unions of three generations of couples living together: grandparents, parents and children. A lawyer works with them to arrange for the civil marriages – he gives his time free. When they have received the sacrament of matrimony, the couples are so happy.'[12]

She was always obedient to the authority of the Catholic Church (Malcolm Muggeridge remarked that it was 'something she accepts in the same unquestioning way that peasants accept the weather, or sailors storms at sea'). Yet if she felt a bishop or priest was not sticking to church teaching – something that became common in the years following Vatican II – she would say so. She once showed a young priest the door when, during a retreat for her sisters, he questioned traditional Catholic teaching about the Eucharist.

CELEBRATIONS

October 1975 marked the twenty-fifth anniversary of the founding of the order. There were now sixty-one Missionaries of Charity houses in India and twenty-seven overseas. To remind the sisters of what their vocation was, the words 'I thirst' were written on the wall of each chapel. The congregation consisted of 1,133 sisters and over 200 novices in three novitiates, in Calcutta, Rome and Melbourne, and over fifty young women a year were applying to join. That might seem a small number, until you consider the huge sacrifice such a life demanded.

In addition, the Co-Workers, headed by Ann Blaikie, had received official recognition from Pope Paul VI in 1969 and now had a worldwide membership of around 80,000.

Mother Teresa liked to divide her congregation's work into five categories: apostolic, medical care, education, social and relief services. Apostolic work included running Sunday schools, Bible study groups and visiting those in prison or hospital. The medical wing consisted of dispensaries, mobile clinics, caring for those with diseases such as leprosy, TB and Aids, and providing homes for abandoned and disabled children. The sisters' educational work involved the running of schools and craft classes. Social work included providing homes for alcoholics, drug addicts and unmarried mothers, as well as night shelters and natural family planning centres. In addition to all of this, the order provided basic relief such as food and clothing.

To mark the anniversary, Lawrence Picachy, who had succeeded Ferdinand Perier as Archbishop of Calcutta, following his death in 1968, celebrated a Mass for the sisters.

Mother Teresa didn't want the anniversary to be just a Catholic celebration, so she took the unusual step of writing to all the religious groups in Calcutta, asking them to hold a service of thanksgiving. Remarkably, they all responded and a list of the services was published in the *Calcutta Post*. Mother Teresa and some of her sisters attended each of the services held by the eighteen groups. In the Moghen Synagogue she recited the 'Magnificat'. At the Jain temple, her arrival was heralded by the sound of cymbals and drums – and, according to tradition, their monks were completely nude.

The week after the celebrations, she flew to North Carolina to pick up another award, the Albert Schweitzer International Prize, and then went on to New York to be the Christian speaker in a spiritual meeting set up by the Temple of Understanding, an interfaith organization. The headline in *The New York Times* read 'Spiritual Parley Hears Living Saint'.

Mother Teresa felt nothing like a saint. Despite the satisfaction she must have felt at the impressive growth of her congregation, and the praise that was heaped upon her, the feelings of God's absence still persisted inside

'In spite of everything Jesus is all to me and...I love no one but only Jesus.'

her. When Malcolm Muggeridge had written to her about his longing for God and his difficulties in believing, she simply encouraged him to persevere and pray, never mentioning her own struggles.

Around this time, she was standing at a bus stop in Rome when a Dutch priest came up to her and introduced himself as Father Michael van der Peet, a member of the Priests of the Sacred Heart. They got chatting and Mother Teresa invited him to come and talk about prayer to some of her novices at a convent on the edge of Rome.

She was impressed and began to write to him for spiritual guidance. Once again, she was describing her spiritual emptiness and darkness, though not with the kind of anxiety she had displayed in her letters to Archbishop Perier, Father Picachy and Father Neuner. This suggests she was coming to accept her doubts; she wrote: 'In spite of everything Jesus is all to me and...I love no one but only Jesus.'[13]

In August 1978, Pope Paul VI died of a heart attack. In one of the shortest conclaves in history, the 111 cardinals surprised everyone by electing as his successor sixty-five-year-old Cardinal Albino Luciani, Patriarch of Venice, who took the name John Paul I. But thirty-three days later, Catholics were stunned by the news that he had been found dead by his private secretary, an event that was to trigger rumours of murder and dark goings-on inside the Vatican.

In October, the cardinals around the world packed their bags again and flew into Rome. This time, there was even more surprise when a smiling fifty-eight-year-old Cardinal Karol Wojtyla, Archbishop of Cracow, appeared on the balcony of St Peter's above the huge, expectant crowd packed into the square below and announced that he had chosen the name

Mother Teresa receiving the Nobel Peace Prize from the Chairman of the Norwegian Nobel Institute, Professor John Sanness, December 1979. The award turned her into an international figure.

Pope John Paul II. The cardinals had elected not only the first non-Italian in 400 years but also a Slav. Catholics in Communist Eastern Europe greeted the news with amazement and excitement.

NOBEL PEACE PRIZE

In 1976, Mother Teresa was given the *Pacem in Terris* Peace and Freedom Award, set up in commemoration of Pope John XXIII's encyclical *Pacem in Terris* ('Peace on Earth'). Previous recipients of the award included Martin Luther King, Jr and Dorothy Day. The money she received went to fund a home for lepers. Glory should not be given to her but to God, she always said, often describing herself as a pencil in God's hand. 'I do nothing. He does it all.'[14]

She had been nominated for the Nobel Peace Prize in 1972, 1975 and 1977, but had been passed over each time. Not that she would have minded. In 1979, aged sixty-nine, she was nominated yet again, and this time the panel voted for her. While she was Catholic through and through, she was also seen as someone who recognized the good in all religions and advocated the kind of inter-religious harmony the Nobel committee supported. For example, she had become a friend and supporter of Brother Roger, who, in 1940, had set up Taizé, an ecumenical community in Burgundy, in France, that attracted thousands of young pilgrims each year. She had learned to appreciate other religions and to see not the differences but the common ground they shared with Christianity.

At the same time, she wasn't prepared to see Christianity sidelined. When the Indian government introduced the Freedom of Religion Bill in 1978 because of concerns that some foreign Christian missionaries were

seeking to convert some Indian groups through free education, medicine and jobs, Mother Teresa reacted by writing a letter to the Prime Minister Morarji Desai, arguing that freedom was only freedom when a person was free to choose his or her religion.

In December 1979, she arrived in Oslo to accept the Nobel Peace Prize, accompanied by Sister Agnes and Sister Gertrude, who had both been with her since the congregation's beginnings. At a reception hosted for her at the Indian Embassy, she told journalists, 'I am myself unworthy of the prize. I do not want it personally. But by this award the Norwegian people have recognized the existence of the poor. It is on their behalf that I have come.'[15] At her request, the traditional banquet was cancelled and the £3,000 used instead to provide meals for the poor.

Amongst those in the audience in the large hall at the University of Oslo were Ann Blaikie, Jacqueline de Decker and her brother, Lazar. Her mother and sister were not there to witness the event. Both had died a few years before.

Professor John Sanness, chairman of the Nobel committee, explained why Mother Teresa had been chosen to receive the prize. 'Mother Teresa works in the world as she finds it, in the slums of Calcutta and other towns and cities. But she makes no distinction between poor and rich persons, between poor and rich countries. Politics has never been her concern.'[16]

Before making her acceptance speech, she invited everyone to recite with her the Prayer of St Francis of Assisi:

'Lord, make me a channel of thy peace; that, where there is hatred, I may bring love; that where there is wrong, I may bring the spirit of forgiveness; that, where there is discord, I may bring harmony; that, where

Mother Teresa in conversation with Brother Roger Shultz, founder of the Taize community, during her pilgrimage to Taize on 23 October 1983. Both emphasised that Christianity was primarily about love.

there is error, I may bring truth; that, where there is doubt, I may bring faith; that, where there is despair, I may bring hope; that, where there are shadows, I may bring light; that, where there is sadness, I may bring joy.

'Lord, grant that I may seek rather to comfort than to be comforted, to understand than to be understood; to love than to be loved; for it is by self-forgetting that one finds; it is by forgiving that one is forgiven; it is by dying that one awakens to eternal life.'

To illustrate the kind of love and sacrifice that she believed the world needed, she told the story of a four-year-old Hindu boy who, hearing that Mother Teresa was finding it difficult to obtain sugar for her homes in Calcutta, told his parents, 'I will not eat sugar for three days, I will give my sugar to Mother Teresa for her children.' By doing this, said Mother Teresa, the boy was making an act of love to those in need.[17]

Mother Teresa then described how her sisters had picked up 36,000 people from the streets of Calcutta and how they also taught natural family planning to Indian women. She spoke of her abhorrence of abortion, telling the audience bluntly, 'If a mother can murder her own child in her own womb, what is left for you and for me but to kill each other?'[18]

Abortion was at this time a highly sensitive issue, thus suggesting Professor Sanness was wrong to say that Mother Teresa never got involved in politics. But for her, abortion wasn't about politics, but human rights and protecting each life that she believed was a gift from God.

Being awarded the Nobel Peace Prize immediately accords one status and increased influence. Mother Teresa was not interested in her own importance, but was soon to discover the effect of this new-found international fame.

Chapter 6

WAR, FAMINE AND DISEASE

During the 1980s, Mother Teresa took maximum advantage of her Nobel status, criss-crossing the globe to start new foundations of her congregation or to dramatically intervene in a disaster zone. She might have been in her seventies, but she seemed to have as much energy as any of the stream of idealistic young backpackers from the West who now turned up at the door of the mother house in Calcutta, seeking to help the sisters serve the poor and, in doing so, perhaps discover some deeper meaning to their lives. Many who hoped to meet Mother Teresa in person were disappointed. If they did meet her, she certainly did not conform to the kind of self-styled spiritual guru India had become famous for. She was more likely to be found sitting patiently in some airport departure lounge, twiddling her rosary.

Mother Teresa now received sacks of letters from people inviting her to give talks or attend conferences (she once quipped that a bishop had told her she would spend purgatory writing letters because she was so bad at answering them). In 1980, she even addressed the Synod of Bishops in Rome, which was rare for a woman. In her typical fashion, she described it as 'being among all the big people of the Church'.[1] The following year she sat down for lunch at the White House with President Ronald Reagan and his wife, Nancy.

Her popularity went far beyond the Catholic Church. She had been presented with the Bharat Ratna, India's highest civilian award, making her the first person born outside India to receive it. Elsewhere, actress Maria Schell reportedly gave her a cheque for $280,000. In *Good Housekeeping* magazine's 1980 poll of its readers, she headed the list of 'most admired women'.

Some of her visits raised a few eyebrows. In 1980, after attending

a natural family planning conference in Guatemala, she flew to Haiti to receive a medal from dictator Jean-Claude – 'Baby Doc' – Duvalier and his wife, Michele. Given the couple's reputation for keeping their subjects in poverty while they squandered millions on their luxury lifestyle, reporters were taken aback when, referring to Mrs Duvalier, Mother Teresa told them 'she had never seen the poor people being so familiar with their head of state as they were with her. It was a beautiful lesson for me. I have learned something from you.'[2] In 1986, she made an unscheduled stop in Cuba and met President Fidel Castro, whose pro-Soviet regime had frosty relations with the Vatican. She still managed to persuade him to allow her sisters to establish a mission in Havana.

Yet her frequent absence from the mother house in Calcutta concerned her, so much so that she asked Pope John Paul II if she should withdraw from public speaking. He wouldn't hear of it, knowing what an incredible advertisement she was for the Catholic Church.

BEIRUT

In August 1982, Mother Teresa decided to travel to Lebanon to visit her six sisters at a school in East Beirut. Because the city was under siege and the air space was controlled by Israeli F16 fighter jets, she was forced to fly to Cyprus and then make the journey to Lebanon by ship. On board with her were Ann and Jeanette Petrie, two Americans to whom she had given permission to make a film about her work.

This small mountainous country at the end of the Mediterranean, sandwiched between Syria and Israel, had been caught up in a civil war since 1975, involving a variety of Christian, Muslim, and Druze militias as well as Israel, Syria and the Palestinian Liberation Organization (PLO). At the heart of the conflict were the Palestinians, who had lost their homes as a result of the 1946-1948 Arab Israeli conflict and the Six Day War in 1967, and many of whom now lived in refugee camps.

Two months before, following the attempted assassination of the Israeli ambassador in London by a Palestinian group, Israeli forces invaded

Lebanon, attacking PLO bases in the south of the country and then sending its tanks towards the capital, Beirut.

Lebanon was unique in the Middle East in having a population that was almost equally split between Muslims and Christians. Politically, the Christians tended to ally themselves with Israel and the West; the Muslims with the Arab states.

Running through the city was what became known as the Green Line, which divided it into the Christian East and the Muslim West. Those who attempted to cross it risked being shot at by snipers or bundled into a car by gunmen and driven away to an uncertain fate.

Since establishing their first foundation in the Middle East in Amman in Jordan, in 1970, the Missionaries of Charity had founded other houses in Gaza, Yemen and, in 1979, in Lebanon.

This was to be Mother Teresa's first time in a war zone. Palls of black smoke and the sound of distant gunfire and heavy thuds greeted her as Beirut's skyline and the mountains behind it came into view. Once ashore, she saw the full horror of the violence. Many of the hotels, shops and apartment blocks in the once elegant streets and tree-lined avenues had been gutted, while charred vehicles lay abandoned alongside piles of refuse. The main road from Beirut to Damascus along the coast had been cut in two by bomb craters. Many of those who hadn't managed to escape the shelling and missile attacks on the city formed long queues for water from taps in the streets.

After visiting her sisters, Mother Teresa was driven across the city past more wrecked buildings to meet Red Cross officials. When she asked them to describe their most serious problem, they told her about a group

An Israeli tank rumbles through a rubble-strewn city street during the Peace for Galilee invasion, 1 Jan 1982. Mother Teresa's rescue attempt with the Red Cross was highly dangerous.

of mentally and physically disabled children and young people who were trapped on the upper floor of Dar al-Ajaza al-Islamia Mental Hospital in West Beirut. Because the home was near a Palestinian refugee camp, missiles had struck it.

Mother Teresa made the kind of snap decision that she was known for, insisting that the children should be taken to her sisters for safety. But to rescue the children would involve crossing the perilous Green Line. Some church leaders advised her against attempting such a rescue, warning her that she might get shot.

Being a nun was no protection in civil wars, as the murder and rape of three American nuns and a lay worker in El Salvador two years before had illustrated. How vulnerable world religious figures had become was brought home in 1981 when a twenty-three-year-old Turk opened fire with a pistol on Pope John Paul II as he blessed the crowds from his popemobile in St Peter's Square. Despite losing several pints of blood and undergoing a five-hour operation, the Pope survived.

Mother Teresa was aware of the dangers, but to her all that mattered were the children. She persuaded the Red Cross to agree to her plan, and a convoy of four vehicles, flying white flags and with sirens blaring, set off across the city. As they drove past bombed-out buildings and groups of armed men, the Red Cross staff knew that they could come under attack at any moment.

When they reached the hospital, they discovered that the windows had been shattered and the two top floors blown apart. Inside, they found thirty-seven frightened and distraught children and young people huddled in a group on the floor amidst the dust and rubble. Along with the Red Cross

Mother Teresa with India's
Prime Minister Indira
Gandhi, New Delhi, 18
November 1972. Mrs
Gandhi admired Mother
Teresa, even though she
held opposing views on
some issues.

workers and remaining hospital staff, Mother Teresa led the hungry and terrified children out of the building to the waiting vehicles. Once through an Israeli checkpoint, the convoy sped through the deserted streets to the convent. As news of the daring rescue spread around the city, locals started arriving with food, clothes, beds and medical help.

Two days later, she took part in a second mission to rescue another group of trapped children.

Afterwards, she commented, 'I have never been in a war before, but I have seen famine and death. I was asking myself, what do they feel when they do this? I don't understand it. They are all children of God. Why do they do it? I don't understand.'[3]

A Red Cross worker remarked, 'What stunned everyone was her energy. She saw the problem, fell to her knees, and prayed for a few seconds, and then she was rattling off a list of supplies she needed... We didn't expect a saint to be so efficient.' Another likened her to 'a cross between a military commander and St Francis'.[4]

Her dramatic rescue operation grabbed media headlines around the world. When journalists asked her for a statement, she read out St Francis of Assisi's prayer for peace, as she had done at the Nobel ceremony in Oslo. But peace was a long way off. The following month, Christian militia stormed two Palestinian refugee camps, massacring hundreds of men, women and children.

In October 1984, the Indian prime minister, Indira Gandhi, was gunned down by members of her Sikh bodyguards in revenge for ordering Indian troops in June to storm the Golden Temple in Amritsar, the Sikhs' holiest shrine.

Mother Teresa was among the international dignitaries who attended Gandhi's cremation in New Delhi. She and Gandhi had shared a mutual respect for one another, despite their different religious beliefs and their disagreement on issues such as abortion, family planning and sterilization. They had first met in 1964 when Gandhi visited Mother Teresa in a nursing home where she was recuperating following a car accident on a road near Darjeeling. In 1973, Gandhi had given her a free pass for Indian Airlines and, in 1976, had presented her with an honorary doctorate at Visva Bharati University.

HIV AND AIDS

In the West, a new killer disease had been detected: HIV/Aids. The first cases were reported among homosexuals in the USA in 1981. It soon emerged that, apart from homosexuals, other groups had a high risk of contracting the virus, including intravenous drug users and their sexual partners and those who shared needles.

There was a lot of ignorance surrounding the disease. Many people believed that it could be contracted from toilet seats, towels and from cups touched by someone who was infected.

Mother Teresa first learned about the devastating impact of HIV/Aids in June 1985 when she visited patients at George Washington University Hospital in Washington DC.

Some church groups delighted in seeing the virus as God's judgment on homosexuals. What Mother Teresa thought privately about a disease that was, in the West at least, often linked to sexual practices that the Catholic Church taught were unnatural, we don't know. But it's reasonable to assume that, on a spiritual level, she must have seen this new disease as a consequence of a world that was abandoning God.

When she made a visit to Sing Sing maximum security prison on the banks of the Hudson River, near New York, she met Antonio Rivera, Jimmy Matos and Daryl Monsett, three men convicted of violent offences. Each of them was also now dying of Aids.

Mother Teresa immediately phoned New York State Governor Mario Cuomo and asked him to transfer the men to a hospital, where they could receive better care. Although he had rejected other appeals made on behalf of the men, he agreed to her request, perhaps thinking that to refuse the request of a Nobel Peace Prize winner hailed as a living saint could cause enormous damage to his political credibility. Within twenty-four hours, the men were admitted to a Manhattan hospital.

When Mother Teresa had an idea, she was impatient to put it into action. Her visit to the patients in George Washington University Hospital and meeting the three prisoners made her realize that those with Aids needed the kind of loving and supportive home that she believed her sisters could provide. If HIV/Aids had indeed become the new leprosy of the West, as some suggested, then she would set about providing care for those who found themselves rejected, just as she had done for those suffering from leprosy in Calcutta.

On Christmas Eve 1985, she opened the Gift of Love Aids hospice in a former rectory in Greenwich Village in downtown Manhattan, with accommodation for fourteen men. The following year, at the invitation of Archbishop James Hickey, she opened a second Aids hospice in a former convent in a leafy middle-class suburb in north-east Washington, DC. The archdiocese had stressed that the Missionaries of Charity house would be primarily a religious community, not a medical facility. However, unlike in Greenwich Village, she had to face fierce local opposition to her plan from some local residents. According to Kathryn Spink in *Mother Teresa: An Authorized Biography* some residents believed Aids could be transmitted through the air. 'One resident of the neighbourhood even protested that a used Kleenex tissue could fall out of the rubbish, blow into her garden and be picked up by her daughter, who might then contract the disease.'[5] Other objections were raised against the hospice. It could lower property prices. And it was going to house homosexuals.

The hospice proposal, however, had some powerful and influential supporters, including the Surgeon General of the US, the director of the National Institute for Infectious Diseases and the Jesuit-run Georgetown University Medical Center. The Gift of Peace hospice went ahead, receiving its first patients from local hospitals in November.

Speaking about her work with HIV/Aids patients, Mother Teresa said, 'We are not here to sit in judgment on these people, to decide blame or guilt. Our mission is to help them, to make their dying days more tolerable.'[6]

To those who claimed that the state could do what her sisters were doing, Mother Teresa once said, 'The state can provide many things – except tender love and care. And not only that. We are not social workers; we may be doing social work but we are not social workers because we are really

Having spent so many years in Calcutta, Mother Teresa was no stranger to the suffering caused by hunger, but she had probably never witnessed it on such a scale as she did when she flew to Ethiopia in 1985.

trying to be contemplatives right in the heart of the world and because we take Christ at his word. He said, "You did it to me." And so we are touching him twenty-four hours a day.'[7]

As Mother Teresa neared her seventy-fifth birthday, she wrote to her sisters asking them to elect someone else as general superior, saying that she just wanted to be a 'simple sister'. But her wish was ignored, and she was re-elected.

Age had not entirely banished her feeling of being distant from God. She told Belgian Jesuit Father Albert Huart, who led a retreat before the general chapter, that while she was able to talk to her sisters and others about the love of God, she felt cut off from God. It was a contradiction she had still not fully accepted.

Someone else who had wrestled with God had finally found resolution. In 1982, aged seventy-nine, Malcolm Muggeridge was received into the Catholic Church, describing it as a homecoming. He wrote, 'In our spiritual lives, I suppose, some sort of subterranean process takes place whereby after years of doubt and uncertainty, clarification and certainty suddenly emerge, and like the blind man whose sight was restored, we say, "One thing I know, that, whereas I was blind, now I see." '[8]

ETHIOPIA

Having spent so many years in Calcutta, Mother Teresa was no stranger to the suffering caused by hunger, but she had probably never witnessed it on such a scale as she did when she flew to Ethiopia in 1985. The Missionaries of Charity had been working there since opening a house in Addis Ababa in

1973. Three more houses had followed, along with a group of sisters who lived in a camp for displaced people.

Poor spring rainfall in the north of the country along with disease had caused a harvest failure, leading the Marxist-led government to warn in March 1984 that five million people were at risk from starvation. It claimed the country could produce only 6.2 million tonnes of grain a year, a million less than was needed. To compound matters, the country was caught up in a civil war.

In October 1984, BBC journalist Michael Buerk had sent back film of what he called a 'biblical famine'. Images of malnourished children, people scrabbling on the ground for grains of rice and hordes marching hundreds of miles across dry land in search of food shocked the Western public and forced governments to act. In a haunting phrase, Buerk said of his visit to Korem in the north of the country, 'This place, say workers here, is the closest thing to hell on earth.'[9]

Western governments and the EU were slow to offer help. What made this even more damning was that Europe, by contrast, had enjoyed a bumper harvest.

Mother Teresa called on the West to adopt the camps the Ethiopian government had set up to resettle the huge numbers who had left their homes in search of food. Such was her influence now that she was able to telephone US President Ronald Reagan at the White House. She described the disaster and pleaded with him for emergency food, medicine and other essentials to be sent. She had always believed the richer nations had a moral responsibility to help the poorer nations, something that had been the key idea in Pope Paul VI's 1967 encyclical *Populorum Progressio*.

It was pop stars rather than politicians who responded most decisively to the images of the starving in Ethiopia. One artist in particular was outraged by the images of suffering in Buerk's report: Bob Geldof, the lead singer in the Irish band Boomtown Rats. He became a rebel who had found a cause. Sounding like an angry Old Testament prophet, he announced that he was going to host a huge pop concert to raise money for the famine victims. In preparation, he assembled an impressive array of top European pop acts, including Sting, Phil Collins, David Bowie and Bono, to form Band Aid and record a charity pop single 'Do They Know It's Christmas?'

Mother Teresa and Geldof met by chance in the departure lounge at Addis Ababa airport. They must have looked an odd couple: she, a wrinkled elderly woman wrapped in a sari; he, the unshaven, tousle-haired arrogant rock star with a penchant for swearing.

Although brought up a Catholic and educated at a private Catholic boarding school near Dublin, Geldof was highly critical of the Catholic Church. One might have therefore expected a certain coolness when he met Mother Teresa. Instead, he saw her as 'the living embodiment of moral good.' His description of her was perceptive: 'There was nothing otherworldly or divine about her. The way she spoke to the journalists showed her to be as deft a manipulator of media as any high-powered PR expert. She does a sort

A chance meeting between two influential people who responded to the Ethiopian famine crisis. Bob Geldof and Mother Teresa met in Addis Ababa airport on 7 January 1985. He arrived to supervise spending £6m from the sales of his BAND AID single, 'Do They Know It's Christmas?.'

'There was nothing otherworldly or divine about her. The way she spoke to the journalists showed her to be as deft a manipulator of media as any high-powered PR expert.'

of "Oh dear, I'm just a frail old lady" shtick. She was outrageously brilliant. There was no false modesty about her and there was a certainty of purpose which left her little patience.'[10]

In July 1985, Geldof staged two Live Aid concerts, one at Wembley Stadium in London and one at JFK Stadium in Philadelphia. These were broadcast on television around the world, attracting an audience, it was claimed, of 1.5 million in 160 countries and raising around £40,000,000 for Ethiopia.

The Missionaries of Charity continued to grow. In 1986, twenty-six new houses were opened in seventeen countries, including Poland, Greece, Japan, Sudan, Canada, Puerto Rica and Cuba. The congregation of priests, the Missionaries of Charity Fathers, also expanded and opened a house in the South Bronx.

To make running such a vast operation easier, Mother Teresa had divided the congregation up into twelve regions. Her goal was to have a house in every country of the world. Like a general plotting a campaign, she would pore over a map, looking at the countries where her sisters were not present.

Her travels were not without serious incident. In October 1986, she was in Tabora, Tanzania, to see seven of her sisters take their final vows. From there, she had planned to fly to Sudan to open houses for victims of the civil war in the south of the country. As her chartered plane was about to take off from an airstrip, it ploughed into a crowd who had gathered to see her off. Three children, a Missionary of Charity sister, and the manager of a leprosy centre were all killed.

POPE JOHN PAUL II VISITS INDIA

In 1986, Pope John Paul II made a pastoral visit to India, twenty-two years after that of Pope Paul VI. He arrived in Calcutta on the third day of his visit. Mother Teresa was there to greet him when he came to visit the Nirmal Hriday home for the dying. When the popemobile arrived, she climbed into it and bent down to kiss his hand. He kissed the top of her head. Beaming, she then led him to meet the head of the Kali temple before draping a garland around his neck.

The Pope went among the sick and dying, embracing some of them and blessing others. The expression on his face showed how affected he was by what he saw. After returning to Rome, he immediately invited the Missionaries of Charity to set up a hospice in the Vatican.

George Weigel recounts in *Witness to Hope*, his authorized biography of Pope John Paul II, 'The managers of popes had said that this was impossible. How could you introduce the poor and vagrants into the Vatican? What about security? John Paul kept pressing and a solution was finally found – to take over and renovate a building on the edge of Vatican City State, beside the Congregation for the Doctrine of the Faith but still within the Vatican walls.'[11]

In June 1987, Pope John Paul II blessed the cornerstone of the house named Gift of Mary, House of Welcome for the Poorest, and it opened the following year. It included male and female dormitories for seventy people, along with a dining room and kitchen to feed a hundred homeless people each day.

Pope John-Paul II visited
India in 1986 and was
deeply moved by his
visit to Nirmal Hriday.

EASTERN EUROPE

Mother Teresa, of course, was an Eastern European. This was easy to forget, as her sari and accent made her seem Indian. She was nearly always referred to as 'Mother Teresa of Calcutta'. She once remarked, 'By blood and origin I am all Albanian. My citizenship is Indian. I am a Catholic nun. As to my calling, I belong to the whole world. As to my heart, I belong entirely to the heart of Jesus.'[12] Both her homelands of Macedonia and Albania were under Communist rule.

Some were surprised that she never joined Pope John Paul II in speaking out against communism and its atheistic ideology. Yet that would have meant becoming involved in international politics, which she didn't see as part of her calling.

It is ironic that the first state in the world to ban religion and declare itself atheistic was Albania, in 1967; a country that could also lay claim to one of the greatest religious figures of the century. Dictator Enver Hoxha was brutal in his crackdown on religion, banning worship and shutting down or destroying churches,

Mother Teresa addresses a group of children during mass at a church in Tirane, Albania.

monasteries and mosques. The Catholic cathedral in the northern city of Shkoder was turned into a sports hall. Dozens of priests and imams were imprisoned or executed.

In contrast, the people of Macedonia were proud that one of their citizens had been awarded the Nobel Peace Prize. When Mother Teresa had visited Skopje in 1970 as a guest of the Red Cross, she had still been largely unknown. In 1980, she arrived as a guest of the city council and was given the red carpet treatment. Not long after, four of her sisters – two Indian, one Maltese and one Albanian – arrived in a run-down district of the city to set up a community, her first behind the Iron Curtain.

In December 1987, Mother Teresa flew into Moscow, emerging from the plane carrying a statue of Mary wrapped in white cotton. This must have puzzled the waiting dignitaries. They would have been unlikely to know that she, like many Catholics, believed that the Virgin Mary had appeared to three children at Fatima in Portugal in 1917 and had asked for the consecration of Russia to her immaculate heart, meaning that she wanted the Pope to ask her to pray for the conversion of the Russian people. By taking a statue of the Virgin Mary with her to Russia, Mother Teresa was signalling her devotion to Mary and acknowledgment of the importance of her message at Fatima.

Travelling with Mother Teresa were Ann and Jeanette Petrie. Mother Teresa had been invited to Russia by the Soviet authorities as a direct result of their film of her life winning a prize at a Moscow film festival. It had taken the Petrie sisters five years to make the film and had involved accompanying Mother Teresa on trips to ten countries.

The next day, she attended Mass at the city's Catholic cathedral, met

with Orthodox leaders and then flew on to Kiev, the Ukrainian capital. Officials then took her to meet some of the families who had been evacuated following the devastating explosion at the Chernobyl nuclear power plant reactor.

In December 1988, she was in Moscow again, this time to sign an agreement with the Soviet authorities to establish a house in the city. It was arranged that the sisters would initially live in an old hospital until they found an apartment.

From Moscow she flew to Armenia, which a few days before had been hit by a massive earthquake, leaving 45,000 dead and 500,000 homeless. She was taken to the city of Leninakan, where most of the apartment blocks had collapsed, some burying their occupants alive. She met with the Soviet prime minister, Nikolai Ryzhkov, and offered to send some of her sisters to help the victims. The following week, four sisters, accompanied by a priest, arrived in the industrial town of Spitak, much of which had been destroyed by the earthquake and many of whose 50,000 inhabitants had been killed.

Having now made inroads into Eastern Europe, Mother Teresa was keen to press home her advantage. She established a second community in Moscow and one in Georgia. An orphanage in Romania for children with Aids, a soup kitchen in Budapest and a house in what was then Czechoslovakia soon followed.

In 1989, she visited Albania, after receiving an invitation from Ramiz Alia, who had succeeded dictator Enver Hoxha as president in 1985. By inviting her, the Albanian government was letting the world know that it was relaxing its hard-line approach to religion, a point further made the following year when the first Mass was celebrated in public since Albania declared itself the world's first atheistic state. The priest who officiated was the archbishop of Shkoder, Simuni Yubani, who had spent the previous twenty-two years in prison for defying the ban on public worship.

As well as visiting clinics and nurseries, Mother Teresa was also taken to the Martyrs' Cemetery on a hill above the capital, Tirana. Standing alongside Hoxha's widow, she placed a wreath on his tomb. This might have seemed surprising, given the terrible crimes Hoxha committed against the Catholic Church. Was her decision to do this a symbolic act of forgiveness? Or was it possibly an attempt to soften up the Albanian government into agreeing to allow her sisters into the country? Whatever her motives were, Mother Teresa left Albania with the government's permission to open two houses. When she returned for the visit of Pope John Paul II in 1993, she had seven houses up and running.

THE FAR EAST

At this time, the world was divided not just by the Iron Curtain but also by the Bamboo Curtain. Mother Teresa was first and foremost a missionary. Like the Jesuits Matteo Ricci and St Francis Xavier 400 years before, she saw the Far East as a frontier to be crossed. She had gained a foothold in the region, establishing six houses in the Philippines, five in Papua New

*When one of the top
officials asked her,
'What is a communist
to you?' she replied,
'A child of God.'*

Guinea and others in Hong Kong, Macau, South Korea, Taiwan and Japan. However, her dream was to open a house in China, something she had expressed to Pope Paul VI in 1969.

In 1985, she received her first invitation to visit China. It came from the Catholic Patriotic Association, which had been created by the Chinese communist government in 1957. This organization had divided the Catholic Church between those who stayed loyal to the Vatican – the underground church – and those who gave allegiance to the unofficial church that ordained bishops without Rome's approval.

During Mother Teresa's four days in the country, she visited an elderly people's home in Peking, a factory employing workers who were disabled and she attended Mass. She also met Deng Pufang, founder of the China Disabled Persons' Federation and the son of the former general secretary of the Communist Party, Deng Xiaoping. When one of the top officials asked her, 'What is a communist to you?' she replied, 'A child of God.'[13] The following morning, the Chinese newspapers reported that Mother Teresa said communists are children of God. As she later told a journalist, she was happy because after a long time the name God had been printed in the papers in China.

FAILING HEALTH

Despite being in her seventies, Mother Teresa had displayed incredible energy, zest and determination in establishing new foundations across the world and bringing her message of love and compassion to the world's disaster zones. Yet her health was starting to fail.

In 1983, while staying in her sisters' convent on Coelian Hill in Rome, she was admitted to the Salvator Mundi Hospital. After a month there, she was then transferred to the Gemelli Hospital, the large Catholic teaching hospital where Pope John Paul II had been treated after the assassination attempt in 1981. A doctor told the world's media that she was being treated for poor blood circulation and had been given painkillers. Whether she had suffered a heart attack, as some newspaper reports suggested, seems unclear.

In September 1989, soon after returning to Calcutta following a brief visit to Albania, where she had met with the president to discuss opening another house there, she was admitted to Woodlands Nursing Home, where doctors diagnosed a blockage in her heart. It seems this was due, in part, to malaria parasites.

The heart specialist who had treated her in Rome six years earlier was flown in, and she was fitted with a temporary pacemaker. In October, she returned to the mother house, but a few weeks later she was back in the nursing home after experiencing spells of dizziness. She underwent major surgery and was fitted with a permanent pacemaker.

Because of her worsening condition, she wrote to Pope John Paul II, asking to resign as head of the Missionaries of Charity and for the general chapter, scheduled for 1991, to be brought forward by a year. In September 1990, the senior sisters from her twelve regions arrived in Calcutta to vote

A Sister of Charity prays for the recovery of Mother Teresa after she underwent major heart surgery, 17 September 1989.

for the next superior general. The congregation had now grown to around 3,500 members and ran 425 houses in 95 countries. Houses in Grenada and Ethiopia had opened the previous month and plans were in place for a hospice in Cambodia for children with HIV/Aids.

With the election of a pope, journalists could debate the runners and riders and speculate on a likely outcome. But the Missionaries of Charity was synonymous with Mother Teresa. Her other sisters, unlike cardinals, were virtually unknown to the wider world. Yet there was some surprise when it was announced that Mother Teresa had been re-elected. In her typically pragmatic and understated way, she told reporters, 'If this is God's will, I will serve in the way God wants.'

Rescuing children caught up in a civil war, setting up Aids hospices, helping famine victims in Ethiopia – few could criticize her for this sort of work. Her views on women and sex, however, were a different matter.

Chapter 7
LOVE AND SEX

While Mother Teresa went unchallenged when she spoke up for the poor in India, Ethiopia and elsewhere, her stand against abortion was more controversial. In her view, the unborn were also the poorest of the poor. Life, she had always reminded those who would listen, began at conception. She believed a foetus was not a blob but a person, and as such was sacred, because it was created by God. She refused to accept the argument that a woman's rights overrode those of the child in her womb, believing no woman had a right to take another life. As her acceptance speech at the Nobel ceremony in Oslo showed, being unpopular never concerned her. Believing abortion was not a political issue but a human rights issue, she repeated her message again in a speech at the UN General Assembly in New York in 1985.

Those who oppose abortion on the grounds that they are pro-life are often criticized for not giving the same value to other forms of life: the poor, abandoned babies and children, and those who become victims of wars. This charge of moral inconsistency could not be levelled at her. What's more, she was a pacifist. In fact, the only Catholic teaching that she is known to have rejected was the theory of the just war.

That said, she drew criticism from some quarters for not speaking out on other issues. According to *The New York Times*, when journalists asked her to comment on apartheid during a visit to the Khayelitsha black township near Cape Town in 1988, she side-stepped the question. While no one would ever suggest that she supported the racist policies of the South African government, some thought that she should have used the opportunity in the township to speak out against it with the same fervour that she frequently did about abortion.

ABORTION

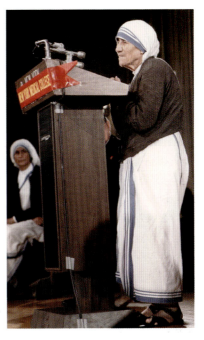

In the West, the pendulum had begun to swing in favour of abortion. Militant feminists, supported by organizations such as International Planned Parenthood, were on a global crusade to have abortion legalized. Denying a woman an abortion, they argued, was denying her control over her own body. Abortion was about the rights and freedom of a woman to choose. The UK legalized abortion in 1967, Canada in 1969, the USA in 1973, and France and Austria in 1975. Italy, the most Catholic country in the world, went the same way in 1978, permitting abortions in the first ninety days of pregnancy.

On the other hand, it was a different picture in Eastern Europe, Africa, Latin America and Asia. While some countries did permit abortion on the grounds of saving a woman's life, protecting her physical or mental health, or in some cases after rape, unlike in North America and parts of Western Europe, it was not allowed for purely socio-economic reasons, which accounted for the vast majority of abortions in the West. India, however, had legalized abortion in 1971.

When Britain made abortion legal in 1967, the intention had been to limit it to pregnancies of up to twenty-eight weeks. Over the years, however, this had been ignored and many people believed the country now effectively operated abortion on demand. Around 2.6 million abortions had been carried out since the Act was passed.

Mother Teresa arrived in London in 1988 at the same time that Liberal Democrat MP David Alton was trying to change Britain's abortion law. He had introduced a Private Member's Bill in Parliament to reduce the time limit for abortions from twenty-eight weeks to eighteen weeks.

For the press, her visit to 10 Downing Street to meet Prime Minister Margaret Thatcher (who had begun office in 1979 by reading out the Prayer of St Francis of Assisi) was a fantastic photo opportunity. Mrs Thatcher voted for the legalization of abortion in 1967, but she was in favour of amending the law, which she thought had become too lax. However, she did not agree with Mother Teresa that abortion was murder.

Mother Teresa spoke to Mrs Thatcher in her usual heartfelt way about both abortion and the plight of those she had seen living on the streets when she had accompanied workers from the Simon Community to what was known as 'Cardboard City' near Waterloo Station, just a few minutes' walk from the Houses of Parliament. She had told journalists afterwards, 'It hurt me so much to see our people in the terrible cold with just a bit of cardboard covering them,'[1] adding that she found poverty in a rich country harder to deal with than poverty in a poor country.

Alton must have been delighted to have Mother Teresa sitting alongside him at a press conference in the House of Commons and seen her presence as a great boost to his campaign. But in the end, because of parliamentary procedures, his attempt to reform the legislation failed. In fact, Mother Teresa's entry into the political debate might well have been counter-productive. The fact that Cardinal Basil Hume, the archbishop of Westminster, and his fellow Catholic bishops were backing Alton, led some to conclude that this was an attempt to impose Catholic teaching on a secular liberal democracy. The sight of Mother Teresa entering the House of Commons must have only reinforced this.

As abortion began to rise up the global political agenda, Mother Teresa responded by making urgent pleas, believing that these might touch the hearts of those involved in political decision-making.

In 1993, she landed by helicopter at the Marian shrine of Knock in County Galway, Ireland. With Mother Teresa sitting nearby, a bishop told the crowds that 'no woman has made such an impact here since Our Lady herself appeared in 1879'.[2] Such a comparison must have acutely embarrassed her, not least because of the questions that constantly plagued her about God and the authenticity of her faith.

For the Irish bishops, she was their secret weapon in the abortion debate. Abortion had become a hot issue after the attorney general had secured an injunction to prevent a 14-year-old rape victim from travelling to England for an abortion only to have it lifted by the Supreme Court because the girl had threatened to commit suicide.

As in many other parts of Catholic Europe, attitudes in Ireland to sexual behaviour were changing, and the voice of the church was being drowned out. Sex outside marriage, contraception and divorce were now becoming the norm amongst the population. Shortly before Mother Teresa's visit, the Irish parliament had voted to allow vending machines selling condoms to be installed in bars and other public places. As recently as the 1970s, 90 per cent of the Irish identified themselves as Catholic and almost the same number went to Mass at least once a week. When Pope John Paul II visited the country in 1979 cheering crowds greeted him, but by the early 1990s, Mass attendance was plummeting, the convents closing and the seminaries emptying. In 1992, Bishop Eamon Casey of Galway and Kilmacduagh resigned after it emerged that he had fathered a son with an American divorcee. At the same time, cases of sexual abuse by priests were beginning to surface for the first time, as they were doing in the US and elsewhere, undermining the moral authority of the Catholic Church.

In 1994, Mother Teresa sent a message to delegates at the International Conference on Population and Development in Cairo, describing abortion as the greatest destroyer of peace in the world and offering to find homes for unwanted children. She went on, 'If all the money that is being spent on finding ways to kill people was used instead to feed them and house them and educate them – how beautiful that world would be.'[3]

Nowhere was abortion more of a highly charged political issue than in the US. While President Ronald Reagan had cut off funds for abortion programmes run by groups such as the International Planned Parenthood Federation and Family Planning International Assistance, Bill Clinton supported their work.

Some anti-abortion groups had decided to take a more aggressive approach by firebombing clinics that carried out abortions and targeting the doctors who performed them. In 1993, Rachelle 'Shelley' Shannon was sentenced to eleven years in prison for shooting a doctor outside an abortion clinic in Wichita, Kansas, and was given another twenty years for firebombing other clinics across western America.

The Catholic Church became embroiled in controversy in 1984 when Cardinal John O'Connor of New York publicly chastised Democratic vice-presidential nominee Geraldine Ferraro for saying there was 'a diversity of Catholic opinion' about abortion.

In 1994, Mother Teresa was invited to be one of the seven guest speakers at the National Prayer Breakfast in Washington, DC. Established in 1953 by a wealthy group of influential Christians, the annual event attracted some 3,000 dignitaries from around the world, each willing to stump up several hundred dollars for the privilege of attending.

When she mounted the podium in the ballroom of the Hilton Hotel, she began by reminding those seated in front of her of Jesus' command to help the hungry, the thirsty and the sick, inviting everyone to join her in reciting the Prayer of St Francis of Assisi, which by now had become her signature tune.

She then told them about the time she had visited a home for the elderly. 'I saw that in that home these old people had everything – good food, a comfortable place, television, everything, but everyone was looking toward the door. And I did not see a single one with a smile on their face. I turned to Sister and I asked, "Why do these people who have every comfort here, why are they all looking toward the door? Why are they not smiling?" And Sister said, "This is the way it is nearly every day. They are expecting, they are hoping, that a son or daughter will come to visit them. They are hurt because they are forgotten." '[4]

There could have been few of those listening to her who were not moved by this story. This would not be the case when she went on to talk about abortion.

She told them, 'But I feel that the greatest destroyer of peace today is abortion, because it is a war against the child, a direct killing of the innocent child, murder by the mother herself. And if we accept that a mother can kill even her own child, how can we tell other people not to kill one another? How do we persuade a woman not to have an abortion?'[5] Her answer was that this should be done with love, not condemnation.

She went on to talk about how adoption was one of her ways of fighting abortion, adding, 'But I never give a child to a couple who have done something not to have a child.'[6] That last line was to remind the audience that she believed contraception was, in God's eyes, just as morally wrong as abortion.

Her policy of allowing children to be adopted by couples overseas had drawn criticism from some. There had been accusations that she was selling Indian children, leading to talk of 'nun running'. At one point, the Indian government had banned her from giving children to overseas couples.

Among the guests listening to Mother Teresa were President Bill Clinton, First Lady Hillary Clinton, and Vice-President Al Gore, who were all in favour of women's choice. Six months before the Cairo conference, the US government had sent a cable to all diplomatic missions, informing them that 'the United States believes that access to safe, legal and voluntary abortion is a fundamental right of all women' and that the US delegation attending the conference 'will be working for stronger language on the importance of access to abortion services'.

In her autobiography *Living History*, Hillary Clinton recalled Mother Teresa's speech in Washington and spoke warmly of her: 'I remember being struck by how tiny she was and I noticed that she was wearing only socks and sandals in the bitter winter cold. She had just delivered her speech against abortion and she wanted to talk to me. Mother Teresa was unerringly direct. She disagreed with my views on a woman's right to choose and she told me so. Over the years, she sent me dozens of notes and messages with the same gentle entreaty. Mother Teresa never lectured or scolded me; her admonitions were always loving and heartfelt. I had the greatest respect for her opposition to abortion, but I believe that it is dangerous to give any state the power to enforce criminal penalties against women and doctors... I also disagreed with her opposition – and that of the Catholic Church – to birth control.'[7]

Clinton spoke about the common ground they both shared when it came to adoption, which she believed was a better choice for women to make than abortion. When she agreed to help Mother Teresa set up a home for babies in Washington, DC, she experienced the nun's sense of urgency in these sorts of ventures. She wrote: 'When I agreed to assist with the project, Mother Teresa revealed her skills as a relentless lobbyist. If she felt the job was lagging, she wrote letters asking me what progress we had made. She sent emissaries to spur me on. She called me from Vietnam, she

*'Like a happy child, she gripped
my arm in her small, strong
hand and dragged me upstairs
to see the freshly painted
nursery and rows of bassinets
waiting to be filled with
infants. Her enthusiasm was
irresistible.'*

called me from India, always with the same message: When do I get my center for babies?' The home opened in 1995 and Mother Teresa flew in to join Clinton for the opening ceremony.

Clinton felt that she had glimpsed the secret of Mother Teresa's influence. 'Like a happy child, she gripped my arm in her small, strong hand and dragged me upstairs to see the freshly painted nursery and rows of bassinets waiting to be filled with infants. Her enthusiasm was irresistible. By then I fully understood how this humble nun could move nations to her will.'[8]

FAMILY PLANNING

Pope Paul VI's 1968 encyclical *Humanae Vitae*, in which he taught that each sexual act had to be open to the transmission of human life, had split the Catholic Church, and become a symbolic marker between conservative and liberal Catholics.

Pope John Paul II had reiterated this teaching in his 1995 encyclical *Evangelium Vitae* ('Gospel of Life') in which he criticized what he called the 'culture of death', by which he meant abortion, contraception, experimentation on human embryos and euthanasia.

Many claimed that the massive increase in the global population, especially amongst the poor in the so-called developing world, was a watertight reason for artificial contraception. It was wrong, they argued, to condemn already large families to having to find food and clothing for another child. To prevent this, they should be given the means to take control over how many children they had.

India's population growth, for example, was one of the fastest in the world and was a major concern for its government. By 1971, it had reached 548 million, more than double what it had been at the beginning of the twentieth century. It was the first country to introduce a family planning programme but this failed to have much impact on millions of illiterate people. Prime Minister Indira Gandhi's electoral defeat in 1977 was widely linked to efforts to introduce a sterilization programme.

Mother Teresa wrote to Indian Prime Minister Morarji in 1978 to protest against the Freedom of Religion Bill. She was keen to point out how her congregation was helping to keep the population figures down, telling him that the natural family planning programme run by her sisters had helped 11,701 Hindu families, 5,568 Muslim families and 4,341 Christian families, meaning that over 60,000 fewer babies had been born.

She often told audiences that in Calcutta she would contact police stations, hospitals and clinics and offer to take any unwanted children. One time, she quipped, 'There is a joke in Calcutta: "Mother Teresa is always talking about family planning and about abortion, but every day she has more and more children." '[9]

Mother Teresa didn't accept that contraception was necessary because there were too many people on the planet. She believed that there was plenty of room and – looking at the affluence of Western societies – plenty of resources to go round. She concurred with Gandhi, who once said, 'There is enough for everyone's needs but not for everyone's greed.'

Natural family planning was her response to the pill, condoms and other forms of contraception. Some of the Missionaries of Charity had been trained in how to teach this, giving women beads so that they could count

Indian mothers talk with Mother Teresa at her mission in Calcutta. But her views on women were seen as controversial in the West.

the days in their cycle. 'A husband and wife should love and respect each other to be able to practise self-control during the fertile days,' Mother Teresa insisted.[10]

She took the same line when the Catholic position on contraception was questioned regarding HIV/Aids in Africa, where the virus was fast becoming the continent's top killer disease, decimating populations in countries such as Uganda, Kenya and Zimbabwe. Condoms, claimed the Catholic Church's critics, were vital in preventing the spread of the virus. Abstinence, not condoms, was the answer to this, she said.

WOMEN

Mother Teresa's opposition to abortion and contraception needs to be seen in the context of how she saw the purpose and role of women. For her, the perfect image of femininity was not to be found in the writings of someone like Germaine Greer but in the life of the Virgin Mary. It was only because Mary had said yes to God that he was able to bring about the salvation of humanity through the incarnation. For Mother Teresa, being a woman was not about burning your bra, but about burning with the love of Christ. Although she herself had chosen celibacy, she believed that motherhood was the highest calling for a woman and a gift from God. She made this point when she sent a message to the UN's Fourth World Conference on Women held in Beijing in 1995. She also showed no regard for the feminist ideology that sought to eradicate differences between men and women, saying, 'I do not understand why some people are saying that men and women are exactly the same, and are denying the beautiful differences between men and women. All God's gifts are good, but they are not all the same.'[11]

In the same vein, she was against the idea of women becoming priests, despite her sisters in some parts of the world doing everything a priest did, except celebrate Mass and hear confession. Some female nuns, especially in the US, were arguing that the Catholic Church's exclusion of women from the priesthood was more about patriarchy than theology. Their calls became louder after the Church of England took the decision to ordain women to the priesthood in 1992 at its General Synod. In 1994, Pope John Paul II blocked off any possibility of women ever being ordained to the priesthood when he issued his apostolic letter '*Ordinatio Sacerdotalis*'.

The fact that Mother Teresa was totally opposed to women becoming priests didn't stop United Press International running a story in 1984 headlined 'Mother Teresa Approves of Women Priests'. It wasn't true, of course. The story arose out of an interview she had given to an Indian journalist. When she said that the only woman who could ever be considered a priest was Our Lady, he thought she had said 'our ladies'.

It's interesting to note that some religious orders whose members were starting to embrace feminist theology and call for the admission of women to the priesthood were failing to attract applicants; these included the Maryknoll Sisters and her own former order, the Sisters of Loreto (now referred to as the Institute of the Blessed Virgin Mary). Yet Mother Teresa's congregation had little trouble in gaining new recruits. By the mid-1990s she had opened novitiates in Calcutta, Rome, Manila, Nairobi, San Francisco and Poland.

Joining the white and blue army of the Missionaries of Charity was to embrace a rigorous and demanding lifestyle, which left little time for what Western culture called personal space, as one sister explained in Lucinda Vardey's *Mother Teresa: A Simple Path*. 'As a Missionary of Charity sister I don't have many opportunities to be alone. Choosing a life of poverty usually means a lack of privacy – we don't have our own rooms to pray and contemplate alone.'[12]

Inevitably, some sisters did leave the Missionaries of Charity, as they did in every religious congregation. In one year, for example, twelve left, three after their final vows and nine after their first vows. Mother Teresa once said, 'We remain very human. We have our ups and downs.'

After returning to Calcutta from Europe following a meeting of the heads of religious congregations, Mother Teresa remarked, 'They talked only of changing the structures of society, organising things in a different way. It all came to nothing; it did not do something for the poor, or preach Christ to those without religion, to those totally ignorant of God. I was happy when it was all over. They had insisted on my going there, but I felt like a fish out of water.'[13]

Given some of the New Age ideas that were shaping certain religious orders, such as Our Lady of Victory Missionary Sisters (some nuns were even offering massage as part of their spirituality programme), Mother Teresa's response was unsurprising. In 1983, she wrote a letter to the US bishops about the vocation of religious sisters. Quoting St Thérèse of Lisieux, she urged sisters to be obedient to the Pope and the teaching of the Catholic Church. She said, 'There has been much disturbance in the religious life of sisters, all due to misguided advice and zeal.'

To her critics, though, she too was misguided, especially when it came to talking about sex. One of them was to go much further than this. Journalist Christopher Hitchens was to accuse her of being nothing but a dangerous fanatic, promoting Catholic propaganda at the expense of the poor.

Chapter 8

HELL'S ANGEL

I t was an English journalist, Malcolm Muggeridge, who was instrumental in turning Mother Teresa into a world famous symbol of compassion. Twenty-five years later, it was another English journalist, Christopher Hitchens, who set out to destroy this image in a television programme that caused outrage amongst her supporters.

Mother Teresa's simplicity, self-sacrifice and humility served as a counterpoint to a Western culture based on excessive consumption, individualism and, increasingly, the cult of the celebrity. As a result of this she was a gift to the media, who depicted her as a living saint. Her name had even become synonymous with doing good. 'Who do you think you are? Mother Teresa?'

Nevertheless, it was inevitable that, at some point, the tables would turn against her. While some criticisms had surfaced in the media over the years, notably by Germaine Greer and a *National Catholic Reporter* article that questioned why Mother Teresa wasn't doing anything to deal with the causes of poverty, these could be likened to nothing more than sniper fire. Now she was to face a full-scale assault.

Leading the charge was author and journalist Christopher Hitchens, a self-professed atheist, who had left England some years before to pursue his career in the United States, where he wrote for, amongst others, *Vanity Fair* and *Harper's*. He had, in fact, opened fire on Mother Teresa two years previously in an article entitled 'Ghoul of Calcutta'. He had met her during a visit to Calcutta in 1980 when he had visited one of her orphanages. 'As we stood by the tiny cots she turned and said, "This is the way we fight contraception and abortion in Calcutta."'[1] Unimpressed, he came away believing that she was not really concerned with helping the poor

Christopher Hitchens: Mother Teresa's fiercest critic

and disadvantaged but rather with pushing Catholic propaganda.

The producer of Hitchens' documentary was fellow left-wing activist Tariq Ali, while Dr Aroup Chatterjee, who had grown up in Calcutta and later moved to London, led the criticism of Mother Teresa. He believed that she was not as selfless as the media made her out, that she was barely known in Calcutta, and that the care and conditions in the institutions she ran left much to be desired. He was also angry that, because of her, Calcutta had become synonymous in the West with poverty; not, as he felt it should be, with culture and the arts.

The programme, *Hell's Angel*, was broadcast on the UK television station Channel 4 on the evening of 8 November 1994. Hitchens went into battle, displaying his trademark barbed and eloquent style in a commentary peppered with the kind of succinct one-liners Muggeridge excelled at.

Hitchens began by accusing Muggeridge of creating what he called the myth of Mother Teresa, dismissing him as 'an old fraud and mountebank'. Mother Teresa was nothing more than a zealot and a fanatic whose real aim, claimed Hitchens, was to promote a dangerous Catholic agenda: 'If it seems that the saint of Calcutta is never in Calcutta at all, this may be because she operates as the roving ambassador of a highly politicized papacy. Vatican foreign policy has taken her from the shores of Lebanon, where the Roman Catholic militia perpetrated the mass murder of the Sabra and Chatilla camps to Nicaragua, where the cardinal was the patron of the Contras, to Armenia, where she helped

'For someone whose kingdom is not of this earth, Mother Teresa has an easy way with thrones, dominions and powers.'

mother church gain a foothold in the Soviet Union.'[2]

Indian journalist Mihir Bose supported this position in the documentary. 'She's not a party political figure but she's a political figure in the sense that a) she's part of what might be called the Catholic agenda, the broader Christian right agenda. And the Catholic Church has generally been following what's considered a hard line under the present pope. She's part of that agenda. And that's a fairly political agenda. You know, no abortion, opposition to birth control, ideas like that would be contested in the political arena. And the second factor is she is also part of the Western agenda, where the West is still part of the Third World.'[3]

If by promoting a Catholic agenda they meant that she was evangelizing, then they were right. After all, from a young age she had wanted to be a missionary. Recruiting more Catholics was not her goal, though, but rather encouraging people to have a change of mind and heart. That for her was the essence of Christianity.

Viewers were told, 'The Teresa cult is now a missionary multi-national, with an annual turnover in the tens of millions.' To her the convent and the catechism mattered more than the clinic, he said. She was, he claimed, exploiting the vulnerable and suffering and using them as a 'supply of raw material of compassion'. She was the result of a 'profane marrying between tawdry media hype and medieval superstition'.

He went on, 'For someone whose kingdom is not of this earth, Mother Teresa has an easy way with thrones, dominions and powers.' By this he was referring to her accepting the Medal of Freedom from Ronald Reagan, whom he charged with funding death squads in Central America – the same death squads, he emphasized, that had murdered nuns in El

Salvador and Archbishop Oscar Romero. He also attacked her for laying a wreath at the tomb of Albanian dictator Enver Hoxha and praising Haitian dictator Jean-Claude Duvalier and his wife, a couple who squandered millions on themselves while many of the population lived in squalor. 'She may or may not comfort the afflicted,' he concluded, 'but she has certainly never been known to afflict the comfortable,' adding that she seemed to admire the strength of the powerful almost as highly as she recommended the resignation of the poor.[4]

Hitchens was right in saying that Mother Teresa was not outspoken against particular governments. Rightly or wrongly, she never saw taking sides as her role. In 1991, after the Iraqi invasion of Kuwait, she pleaded with both George Bush (Senior) and Saddam Hussein not to go to war. And, with the exception of her embarrassing involvement in the Christian Dalit protest in New Delhi in 1995, she was consistent in her position. She never publicly criticized the Hoxha regime for its persecution of the Catholic Church in Albania, the homeland of her parents. Nor, for that matter, did she become involved in the Kosovo conflict in the late 1990s when Serbs drove ethnic Albanians from their homes.

Shaped by a very traditional Catholicism, Mother Teresa believed that any criticisms of individual governments should be left to the Pope and the bishops. Where she spoke out was on issues such as Western materialism, the need for the rich to help the poor, the need to value and care for the weakest in society, on abortion and on the need for harmony between religions.

Hitchens failed to understand that the reason why she never criticized political leaders was because, no matter how unlikely this might

appear, she believed some good was always to be found in every person and any situation. In this, she was following Jesus, who had also been attacked for mixing with unsavoury characters. She once said, 'My calling is not to judge the institutions. I am not qualified to condemn anyone. I never think in terms of crowds, but of individual persons.'[5]

Hitchens questioned Mother Teresa's morality for accepting money from the controversial and flamboyant newspaper tycoon Robert Maxwell. Not long before he fell overboard and drowned while on board his private yacht in 1991, it emerged that he had used hundreds of millions of pounds from his companies' pension funds to finance his corporate debt, business dealings and extravagant lifestyle. Thousands of his employees were shocked to discover that their pensions had disappeared.

Mother Teresa had met Maxwell during her visit to London in 1988 when she had lent her support to David Alton's campaign to reduce the time limit for abortions. Hitchens observed that 'his genius for self-promotion made a nice fit with Mother Teresa's talent for fundraising'.

Maxwell took her to view a property that he thought might be suitable for a hostel she wanted to open, and then launched an appeal in the *Daily Mirror*. Its readers responded by sending in £169,000, while readers of its Scottish sister paper, the *Daily Record*, sent £90,000. By the time of Maxwell's death, the money had not been sent to the Missionaries

British media proprietor Robert Maxwell urged Daily Mirror readers to support the work of the Missionaries of Charity.

of Charity. The Mirror Group said this was because a property had still not been found. A hostel finally opened five years after the appeal.

Hitchens further claimed that Mother Teresa had accepted a $1.5m donation from Charles Keating, who was convicted in 1992 of one of the biggest financial frauds in US history and sentenced to ten years in prison, a sentence that was later overturned, although Keating was jailed again in 1999 when he pleaded guilty to other fraud charges.

It was true – Mother Teresa had accepted the donation and moreover had written to Judge Lance Ito of the Superior Court in Los Angeles in Keating's defence, explaining that, while she knew nothing of Keating's business affairs, Keating had done much to help the poor.

Hitchens claimed Mother Teresa flew in Keating's private jet and allowed him to 'make use of her prestige on several important occasions and gave him a personalized crucifix which he took everywhere with him'.[6] One wonders what on earth Hitchens expected her to give him.

Malcolm Muggeridge once reportedly said that Mother Teresa would take money from the devil himself if she could use it well. She claimed she never gave money any thought. 'It always comes. The Lord sends it. We do his work; he provides the means. If he does not give us the means, that shows that he does not want the work. So why worry?'[7] She accepted money from anyone. If someone had a dubious reputation, then that act of giving to the poor might lead to him having a change of heart.

What she meant by this was that she relied on what she called God's providence to fund her work. When people offered her donations, she saw this as God providing, such as when PLO leader Yasser Arafat travelled to Calcutta in 1990 to present her with a cheque for $50,000. She never questioned the source of the money. The way she seems to have managed the finances of the order was, by Western standards, perhaps a bit loose, but not even Hitchens alleged that she, or any of her congregation, had siphoned off money to live the jet-set life, a charge that some television evangelists and pastors of mega-churches in the US have had levelled against them, in several cases, justifiably. Unlike the members of some religious orders who claimed to embrace poverty, all the Missionaries of Charity lived a frugal and spartan life and wasted nothing. Mother Teresa might have met the rich, but luxury and excess were not words you would ever associate with her congregation.

Mother Teresa was, in fact, very particular that all the money she received was spent on the poor and the sick. In 1993, she closed down the Co-Workers, because she believed that too much money was being spent on travel and publicity and that the organization had lost its original spirit of simplicity and prayer.

SERIOUS QUESTIONS

While it could be argued that much of the criticism in the documentary was biased and presented from an anti-religious stand-point, Hitchens' accusation that the conditions in some of her congregation's homes were primitive and that the medical care provided was sub-standard was harder to refute.

Author Mary Loudon, who had once worked as a volunteer at the home for the dying in Calcutta, appeared in the programme, accusing Mother Teresa of failing to provide enough drips and sufficiently strong painkillers for those suffering from diseases such as cancer. She claimed that when she asked a sister why needles were being rinsed with cold water instead of sterilized with boiling water, the reply was that there was no point because there was no time. If this happened, it's unclear whether it was common practice amongst all the sisters or an isolated case.

A few weeks before the television broadcast, Dr Robin Fox, editor of the medical journal *The Lancet*, had questioned the standard of medical care at Nirmal Hriday, which he had visited with his wife. He cited the case of a young man who was diagnosed with meningitis but, in fact, died of cerebral malaria. He couldn't understand why none of the staff had looked at a blood film. 'What happens depends on chance; it could be a Dutch or Japanese nurse or even one of the volunteers who do much of the initial assessment and they might not immediately think of cerebral malaria.'[8] He felt more could have been done to make the patients more comfortable and he questioned the competence of the sisters in managing pain.

Others who had worked at Nirmal Hriday had also commented on the medical care provided. Father Paul Chetcuti, a Maltese Jesuit who worked there in the 1980s, wrote of Mother Teresa: 'In her home for the dying in Calcutta, she refuses to employ a full-time doctor and is happy simply to have the free service of one or two doctors who volunteer their time. She refuses all sophisticated equipment in her homes, even a simple microscope which could be useful in the rapid diagnosis of certain sicknesses. In her eyes this would be the first step towards the establishment of an institution for sick people.'[9]

He goes on, referring to the treatment of a female patient, 'Incompetence is not at all excluded; mistakes are made... It does not matter

No organization, not even one run by Mother Teresa, is perfect.

if they do not have the necessary vaccine for the treatment of this woman, because they give her what has been given to them free of charge – the love of God and the few medicines they possess. God will take care of this sick woman. To human eyes this trust in God seems carried to excess, but it is the touchstone of the whole work of Mother Teresa.'[10]

Wendy Bainbridge, a nurse who worked at a Plymouth hospice and decided to spend her annual leave helping at one of Mother Teresa's homes for the dying, was also critical of the way pain was managed and of hygiene standards. Nevertheless, she also said, 'Much happiness was generated between the sisters, volunteers and patients in grim conditions. Emotional comfort was given with hugs, touching or stroking.' She was also impressed with how the patients met death. 'The actual act of dying was quiet and without struggle or the benefit of analgesia or sedation. Spirituality seemed to have an extra dimension which overcame physiological deficits.'[11]

No organization, not even one run by Mother Teresa, is perfect, and it seems that there were sometimes errors of judgment and lax standards of patient care that could justifiably be seen as inexcusable. Mother Teresa drilled into her sisters that suffering was to be embraced, not avoided, because it is a way of sharing in the suffering of Christ, but this was no reason not to provide adequate medical facilities and treatment to those who were sick and dying.

Chatterjee claimed in *Mother Teresa: The Final Verdict* that Mother Teresa even refused to install washing machines in the home for the dying in Calcutta. For her, the importance of spiritual matters outweighed that of physical requirements. When you compare photographs of the home for the dying in Calcutta in the early days with modern times, what's striking

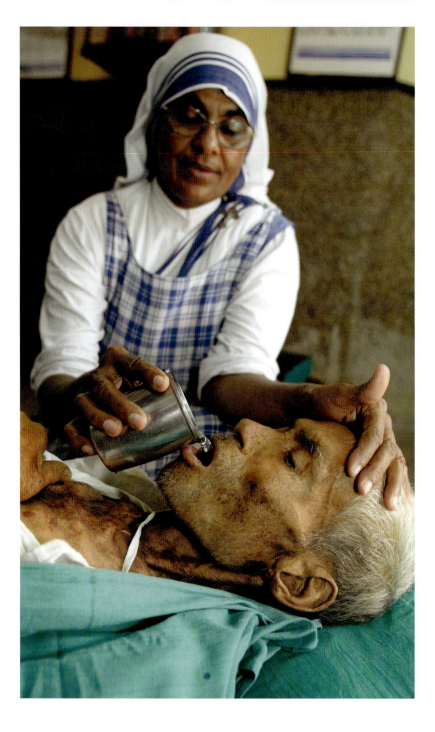

Sister Theresina, the head of the Nirmal Hriday home for the dying and destitute, feeds a seriously ill man.

is that it seems hardly to have changed: the same matchstick figures are lying on the same stretcher beds, all laid out in rows down either side of a spartan large room.

Dr Jack Preger, who once worked with the Missionaries of Charity but left because he felt their standard of care was poor, said that her institutions were run 'on the style of British poor houses 200 years ago. A great deal more should be done in terms of modern medical care. The defence always was we're not a medical order. But if you're involved with sick people and you're not a medical order, you should bring in people who are. That they didn't really accept.'[12]

THE REACTION

Out of the 1.6 million viewers who tuned in to *Hell's Angel*, 130 were outraged enough to formally complain to the watchdog, the Independent Television Commission (ITC). Despite this, it decided to take no action against Channel 4, ruling that the criticisms of Mother Teresa fell within their guidelines of what was fair.

An editorial in the international Catholic weekly *The Tablet*, a publication that was often critical of aspects of the Catholic Church, came to Mother Teresa's defence, accusing Hitchens and Ali of self-righteousness and of misunderstanding and misrepresenting Mother Teresa who, it said, 'stands in an older tradition than that of modern liberation development work, which concentrates on the causes and not only the consequences of poverty: her aid work lays emphasis on binding up the wounds'.

Defending her stance on abortion, the editorial continued, 'Saints also make people uncomfortable. Because of the work she does, Mother Teresa has a particular horror of abortion, which she expresses whenever and wherever she can. Her audiences sometimes do not know where to look, and nor did Channel 4. It is remarkable how in Western society abortion has moved from something that was universally regretted to being the badge of liberalism and political correctness.'[13]

Afterwards, Cardinal Basil Hume, Archbishop of Westminster, described the programme as a 'grotesque caricature', adding, 'she has been able to plead with the rich and powerful on behalf of the poor. Her transparent goodness and practical compassion have, without words, spoken powerfully to millions.'[14]

David Alton MP wrote to Channel 4 chief executive Michael Grade, who defended the programme, saying that the *Without Walls* series, of which the programme was a part, had a 'tradition of allowing individuals the opportunity to present their personal reactions to established icons that would normally receive an unquestionably favourable press'.

The programme was only broadcast in the UK, but once reports of it reached other parts of the world, there was, predictably, similar outrage amongst her supporters.

The following year, an unrepentant Hitchens launched another attack, this time in his book *The Missionary Position: Mother Teresa in theory and practice*. His attempts to discredit her failed once more. Even a disgruntled ex-Missionary of Charity was unable to provide any real firepower. Nevertheless, because the book was translated into several European languages it took his criticisms to a much broader audience, producing dismay as well as debate from her supporters in Italy, France,

Spain, Belgium and elsewhere. And Hitchens continued his attacks, for example in the French publication *Le Monde diplomatique*.

Mother Teresa, however, had more pressing concerns than what Hitchens thought of her. Now in her mid-eighties, her health was fast deteriorating.

Chapter 9
GOING HOME

In June 1997, newspapers around the world carried photographs of a smiling Mother Teresa emerging from her convent on East 145th Street in the Bronx holding hands with the much taller Princess Diana of Wales, dressed in a white suit. The two women stood chatting for a while on the pavement, as the cameras flashed, and then Diana bent down to hug Mother Teresa before waving to the bystanders and getting into her limousine.

It was the perfect image for newspaper editors: the elderly woman proclaimed a living saint with the troubled, beautiful English princess who was herself trying to do good in the world by lending her support to causes, such as Aids and the campaign against land mines. The image was to be given extra poignancy just weeks later when both women died within days of each other.

Mother Teresa and Princess Diana seemed an unlikely pairing. Mother Teresa came from a simple family in the backwaters of Eastern Europe and had spent all her adult life as a nun. She owned nothing and lived among the poorest of the poor. She had no time for frivolity and was appalled by the decadence and triviality of Western culture.

Diana, who was young enough to be her granddaughter, had grown up in an aristocratic family on a country estate in England. Her idyllic childhood was shattered by her parents' divorce when she was eight. In 1981, aged nineteen, she married Prince Charles, the future king of England, in St Paul's Cathedral.

By the time she first met Mother Teresa in 1992, she and Prince Charles had separated and she had become so unhappy that she had attempted suicide.

*Perhaps one of the
reasons why Mother
Teresa seemed to connect
in some way with
Diana was that she saw
that, while Diana was
materially rich, she was
spiritually poor.*

Diana had become intrigued by Mother Teresa. During an official visit to India with Prince Charles, she had visited the Missionaries of Charity headquarters in Calcutta, expecting to meet her, only to be told that she was in hospital in Rome. Diana was given a note from her, apologizing for her absence and expressing her best wishes. Determined to meet her, Diana made an unscheduled stop in Rome on her way back to London and went to see her in hospital.

They met again at the Missionary of Charity house in Kilburn, north-west London, and in 1993 when Mother Teresa was in London to open a hostel for the homeless near St George's Cathedral. This time, Diana invited her to Kensington Palace.

Perhaps one of the reasons why Mother Teresa seemed to connect in some way with Diana was that she saw that, while Diana was materially rich, she was spiritually poor. Maybe the brokenness and rejection Diana felt as the result of her marriage break-up was something Mother Teresa could relate to. She had never been married, of course, but she had for nearly fifty years lived with a feeling of being abandoned by God. Perhaps she could identify with the emptiness that Diana felt.

While a feature on Mother Teresa in the glossy celebrity magazine *Hello!* passed without controversy, the same was not true when, in 1996, Mother Teresa gave an interview to Daphne Barak, who describes herself as 'The only A-list interviewer syndicated worldwide'. Unlike most people Barak interviewed, Mother Teresa didn't have PR advisors. For a journalist more used to carefully managed celebrities, she was a dream.

The interview appeared in the magazine *Ladies' Home Journal*, shortly after it had been announced that Princess Diana and Prince Charles were

Princess Diana bonds with Mother Teresa in New York: an unlikely relationship. They were to die within a week of each other.

to divorce. When Mother Teresa was asked for her reaction to the divorce, Barak claims she replied, 'I think it is a sad story. Diana is such a sad soul. She gives so much love but she needs to get it back. You know what? It is good that it is over. Nobody was happy anyhow.'[1]

These unexpected remarks predictably grabbed newspaper headlines around the world and caused some alarm in the Vatican. Mother Teresa responded swiftly by denying that she had ever advocated divorce when she spoke to Barak. Even if she had secretly thought that the couple's divorce was for the best, she would never have stated that publicly.

If she had been misquoted, it wouldn't have been the first time it had happened. After she attended a Habitat press conference in Vancouver, a story appeared in one newspaper under the headline 'Buy Cheaper Clothes, Eat Less, Mother Teresa Urges Trudeau'. While she had spoken about the need for people to buy cheaper clothes and eat less, she had never mentioned Trudeau, the former Canadian prime minister.

IN HOSPITAL

Ever since being fitted with a pacemaker in 1989, Mother Teresa had suffered from heart problems and also become prone to accidents. By the 1990s she was also suffering from memory loss. In 1991, she had been treated for her heart and also for bacterial pneumonia at Scripps Clinic and Research Foundation in San Diego, California. On a visit to Tijuana in Mexico, she underwent a balloon angioplasty. In 1993, while in Rome, she fell in the bathroom of the convent she was staying in and broke three of her ribs. In August of that year she was taken ill

The eve of Mother Teresa's
funeral, 12 September 1997.
She was mourned by many in
Calcutta.

in Delhi shortly before she was due to receive an award from the Indian government, and she had to spend her eighty-third birthday in hospital, part of it in intensive care.

She was unable to attend the funeral in September of Father Celeste Van Exem, the wise Jesuit who had been her spiritual mentor and helped her and her sisters in those early days in Calcutta. In a note to her, he said he was offering Mass that she might be in China by the following month. At a meeting of Co-Workers in Antwerp, Belgium, earlier that year she had expressed optimism that she would be given permission by the Chinese government to open a house.

Given her poor health, such a trip must have looked unlikely, but within a few weeks she was walking across the tarmac at Shanghai's Hongqiao Airport. She travelled to Beijing, where she met with Deng Pufang and discussed the possibility of opening a home for disabled children. To her disappointment, though, the government refused to give her permission. The following year, she returned to try again, meeting with the archbishop of Shanghai and China Disabled Persons' Federation founder, Deng Pufang, once more. She must have been optimistic of fulfilling her dream of a house in China, but again the government stonewalled her.

Throughout 1996, she was in and out of hospital, but her spirits must have been lifted by the fourteen new houses that opened. These included her first foundations in Crete, Wales, Denmark and Senegal, as well as a return to Northern Ireland when a group of her sisters arrived in Armagh.

In 1997, she was again admitted to Woodlands Nursing Home. When Archbishop Henry D'Souza of Calcutta went to see her, she revealed

to him that she was full of doubts and fears and couldn't sleep. A doctor told him that during the night she became so agitated and restless that she would pull at the wires attached to her. Concerned that an evil spirit might possess her, he asked Father Rosario Stroscio, an Italian Salesian monk, to pray over her.

She had spoken of having no fear of death, seeing it simply as the route back home. In Lucinda Vardey's *Mother Teresa: A Simple Path* she is quoted as saying, 'People ask me about death and whether I look forward to it and I answer, "Of course, because I am going home. Dying is not the end, it is just the beginning. Death is a continuation of life. This is the meaning of eternal life; it is where our souls go to God, to see God, to speak to God… When we die we are going to be with God and with all those we have known who have gone before us: our family and our friends will be there waiting for us. Heaven must be a beautiful place."'[2]

Soon after she was discharged, she was taken back in after another fall and given a brain scan. Two months later, she was rushed to BM Birla Heart Institute in Calcutta where blockages had to be removed from two arteries.

When 120 of her senior sisters met in Calcutta in March 1997 for the general chapter to elect the superior general it was out of the question that Mother Teresa could continue in office. The woman chosen to succeed her was 63-year-old Sister Nirmala Joshi. The daughter of an officer in the Indian army, she had grown up in a wealthy Nepalese family in Duranda in north-east India. Although her family were high-caste Hindus, she had been educated by Christian missionaries. In 1958, at the age of twenty-four, she converted to Catholicism, and in the same year joined the Missionaries of Charity, having heard about Mother Teresa from an American Jesuit. Mother Teresa sent her to the University of Calcutta to gain a law degree so that she could provide free legal help to the poor. She ended up never using this knowledge, going instead to Venezuela to start the congregation's first overseas mission. Later, in 1976, she became head of its first contemplative house in the Bronx.

Displaying extraordinary resilience and stamina, Mother Teresa flew to Rome in May 1997 for the profession of some of her sisters. She also met Pope John Paul II to discuss setting up a house to help the city's prostitutes. In August, against her doctors' advice, she made what was to be her last overseas trip when she flew to Washington, DC to receive the Congressional Gold Medal, the US's highest civilian award, whose recipients included George Washington, the Wright brothers, Walt Disney and Frank Sinatra. From there she went to New York, where she visited her sisters in the Bronx and met Princess Diana.

Mother Teresa seemed to know that death was not far away. Maybe, in part, this was because Sister Agnes, the first to join the Missionaries of Charity, had died a few weeks after the general chapter, and Ann Blaikie and Jacqueline de Decker, two women who had supported her from the

early days, had both died the year before. In July, she told a friend, 'My work is done.'[3]

On 31 August 1997, news broke that 36-year-old Princess Diana had been killed after the Mercedes carrying her and Dodi Al Fayed, son of Harrods' owner Mohammed Al Fayed, crashed in the early hours in a tunnel in the centre of Paris after the couple had enjoyed an evening at the Ritz Hotel.

The morning after, Mother Teresa, sitting in a wheelchair and clutching a photograph of Princess Diana, made a surprise appearance on the balcony of her headquarters in Calcutta. It was to be the last time she was seen in public.

A few days later, a sister came into her room to see her turned towards a picture of Christ and murmuring, 'Jesus, I never refuse you anything.'

On 5 September, she died. After complaining of chest pains, she had been examined by a doctor. She had been due to attend a special prayer service that evening for Princess Diana, but she wasn't strong enough. At 9.30 p.m. she suffered a heart attack and, as she always liked to speak of death, 'went home to God'. The year of her death was coincidentally

the centenary of the death of St Thérèse of Lisieux, who a few weeks later became only the third woman to be made a doctor of the Catholic Church.

A STATE FUNERAL

The announcement from the Indian government that Mother Teresa was to be given a state funeral, an honour usually reserved for heads of state and leading political figures, was condemned by a militant Hindu group. The secretary general of the Vishwa Hindu Parishad, or World Council of Hindus, told a press conference in New Delhi, 'I do not understand why the entirely religious Mother Teresa is being given a state burial when behind her services there was a motive of baptizing.'

This reaction was not surprising, not least because in 1995, Mother Teresa had angered some Hindus by taking part in a prayer service and fast in the Sacred Heart Cathedral in Delhi to demand that Christian Dalits be given access to government jobs that had been until then reserved for low-caste Hindus. At a press conference, she denied knowing that the cathedral service was part of the Dalit protest. This only served to add to the controversy, as it emerged that the auxiliary bishop of Delhi, Vincent Consessao, had briefed her, and also sent her a background paper.

Some of Mother
Teresa's sisters
express their grief
following her death,
6 September 1997.

*Her body was first
taken to St Thomas's
Church, where
thousands came to
pay tribute.*

The Indian government ignored the protests, and plans for the funeral went ahead. It recognized the enormous good she had done in India, and her popularity amongst many in the country. Glamorous Bollywood star Madhuri Dixit and pop singer Usha Uthup were just two of the high-profile Indians who supported her. And far from denigrating Calcutta, as Chatterjee claimed, Mother Teresa had only ever spoken with affection about the city, its culture and its people.

Her body was first taken to St Thomas's Church, where thousands came to paid tribute. It lay there for eight days, during which time media rumours circulated that it had begun to decompose. These were immediately dismissed by the Missionaries of Charity.

On 13 September, eight soldiers in blue caps bore her open coffin out of the church, placing it on the same gun carriage that carried Mahatma Gandhi to his funeral pyre in 1948. It was pulled by a military truck decorated with garlands of jasmine. As the procession made its way through the streets, led by a military band of bagpipers and a contingent of soldiers in red turbans, police had to hold back people trying to touch the coffin. Others threw flower petals as it passed. According to some reports, as many as a million people lined the three-mile procession route to the Netaji indoor stadium.

Amongst the estimated 15,000 mourners inside the stadium were Hillary Clinton, Queen Noor of Jordan, Queen Sofia of Spain, the Italian president, Oscar Scalfaro, Bernadette Chirac of France, Rajiv Ghandi's widow, Sonia, the presidents of Albania and Ghana, and the Duchess of Kent, who represented Queen Elizabeth II.

Despite all the pomp, the Missionaries of Charity asked that half of

The Indian government gave Mother Teresa a state funeral. Calcutta, 13 September 1997.

the seats in the stadium be reserved for the poor and sick. Mother Teresa's coffin was set on a dais and draped in the green, white and saffron tricolour flag of her adopted homeland. She was dressed in her trademark blue-trimmed white sari. Her rosary and a crucifix had been placed in her hands. A large banner on the front of the altar bore the words 'Works of love are works of peace'.

The readings from the Bible were in Bengali and Hindi, while a choir made up of rows of Missionaries of Charity sisters sang various parts of the Mass. At the offertory procession, when the bread, wine and water are taken up to the altar, a leprosy patient carried the wine, a disabled man the bread and a woman released from prison the water.

Cardinal Angelo Sodano, the Vatican's secretary of state, and Pope John Paul's personal representative, celebrated the Mass, along with Archbishop Henry D'Souza of Calcutta and dozens of bishops and priests. He said, 'She taught the world this lesson – it is more blessed to give than to receive.'

Speaking of the criticism some had levelled at her, he said, 'Mother Teresa was aware

of this criticism. She would shrug as if to say, "While you go on discussing causes and explanations, I will kneel beside the poorest of the poor and attend to their needs." '

At the end of the three-hour service, there were messages and prayers from Hindu, Muslim, Sikh, Buddhist, Parsee and Anglican representatives. Her body was then taken to the mother house in Lower Circular Road for a private burial.

Although documentaries about Mother Teresa had been made by Malcolm Muggeridge and the Petrie sisters, she never got to see the first film about her life, *In the Name of God's Poor*. She was played by American actress Geraldine Chaplin (British actress Glenda Jackson had originally been touted for the part, but then thought unsuitable given that she had appeared in sexually explicit films such as *Women in Love*), daughter of screen-legend Charlie Chaplin, and whose credits included the 1965 epic *Doctor Zhivago*. The film was written and produced by Dominique Lapierre, who had worked as a foreign correspondent for *Paris Match* and who had first met Mother Teresa while in Calcutta in the 1980s researching his book *The City of Joy*, which became a best-seller and also a movie. According to Kathryn Spink in *Mother Teresa*: *An Authorized Biography*, in 1982, Mother Teresa had signed an agreement giving him permission to make a movie of her life, but later withdrawn it. After she was assured by the French film-maker that the content of the film would reflect her spiritual aims, she recanted, only to once again withdraw permission. By the time of the film's release on television in America in 1997, she was dying.

Mother Teresa left behind nearly 4,000 Missionaries of Charity sisters and 610 foundations in 123 countries. In their blue-trimmed white saris and white veils they had become not just the most famous order of nuns in the world but also as instantly recognizable as the Beefeaters who guard the Tower of London. Yet they weren't the largest order of religious sisters. For example, the Salesian Sisters numbered over 15,000, the Calced Carmelites nearly 12,000 and both the Franciscan Missionaries of Mary and the Franciscan Clarists around 7,000. But how many people, even Catholics, have ever heard of them, let alone would be able to spot them in the street?

Mother Teresa had also established a contemplative congregation of sisters, two congregations of brothers, one active, one contemplative, and the Missionaries of Charity Fathers. In addition, what was known as the Missionary of Charity family also included the Co-Workers, the Corpus Christi movement of priests, lay missionaries and volunteers.

The question was now: would the Vatican officially make her a saint, and, if so, when?

Chapter 10
SANCTITY AND CELEBRITY

Within weeks of Mother Teresa's death in September 1997, Archbishop Henry D'Souza of Calcutta asked the Vatican's Congregation for the Causes of Saints to lift the usual five-year waiting period and allow her cause for canonization to begin at once. Given Mother Teresa's reputation for holiness, it came as no surprise when in October the permission was granted.

The process of canonization is, in fact, a late development in the Catholic Church. For the first 1,000 years or so, men and women were declared saints not through any formal process but by their contemporaries. To become a saint usually meant having to undergo martyrdom or imprisonment. Later, the term was extended to include those who had simply lived a life of exceptional holiness – the majority of them priests, monks or nuns. Today, two miracles are required in order for the church to proclaim someone a saint.

While some find the whole idea of sainthood somewhat bizarre, the idea actually expresses one of the basic doctrines contained in the Apostles' and Nicene Creeds (statements of faith which the majority of Christians believe in) – that of the communion of saints. In other words, the idea that our lives here on earth are intertwined with those who have passed through death and now live on in the presence of God. Catholics believe that just as Christians ask others to pray for them here on earth, so too can they ask those who are now with God to do the same.

Father Brian Kolodiejchuk, a Canadian Missionaries of Charity Father, was put in charge of the process, a position known as postulator, which began in July 1999 when twelve members of a diocesan enquiry team were sworn in at St Mary's Church, Calcutta. It would be their job to conduct interviews with those who had met Mother Teresa and also to examine her writings.

They spent two years gathering evidence, ending up with eighty 450-page volumes, which were then sent to the Congregation for the Causes of Saints in Rome. Amongst those interviewed were two of her fiercest critics, Christopher Hitchens and Aroup Chatterjee. At the offices of the diocese of Westminster Chatterjee was asked to provide answers to 263 questions about Mother Teresa's life and work.

In September 2001, Associated Press flashed a story around the world that Mother Teresa had undergone an exorcism when Father Rosario Stroscio had visited her in Woodlands Nursing Home, Calcutta, not long before her death in 1997. The source cited was Archbishop D'Souza himself in an interview with the Italian daily *Il Messaggero*. He denied this, claiming that he had been misquoted.

For Mother Teresa to be declared a saint, which would allocate her a feast day in the Catholic Church's liturgical calendar and allow churches and shrines to be dedicated to her, she first had to complete the step of beatification. This required proof of a miracle.

It wasn't long in coming. In June 2002, a panel of medical experts concluded that Monica Besra, who lived in a village some 400 miles north-east of Calcutta, had been cured of stomach cancer through praying to Mother Teresa in 1988. Their findings were then examined by two groups of theologians and eventually ratified by the Congregation for the Causes of Saints.

In front of a packed St Peter's Square, Pope John Paul II beatified Mother Teresa on 19 October 2003, who now became Blessed Mother Teresa. Her canonization had been brought one step closer.

Pope John Paul II leaves St. Peter's Square at the end of the beatification ceremony of Mother Teresa, 19 October 2003 in Vatican City, Italy. Mother Teresa will now be known as the Blessed Mother Teresa of Kolkata, one step away from sainthood.

'God is everywhere and in everything and without him we cannot exist. I have never for one moment doubted the existence of God but I know some people do.'

POPE JOHN PAUL II AND MOTHER TERESA

Mother Teresa and Pope John Paul II both saw themselves as missionaries and wanted to take the gospel to the furthest outpost. George Weigel, Pope John Paul's official biographer, observed: 'Whenever they met (which was usually in Rome), the nun wanted to talk about how her community, the Missionaries of Charity, was expanding. "I have started a house in Russia," or "I have started a house in China."'[1]

In fact, Mother Teresa's wish to open a house in China was never fulfilled, but she made three trips there. When Pope John Paul II died in 2005, two of his goals remained unaccomplished: to visit China and Russia. By contrast, Mother Teresa had made several journeys to Russia. Furthermore, she also visited Iraq in 1991, something the Pope had wanted to do in the jubilee year of 2000 as part of his pilgrimage in the footsteps of Abraham, but the trip was cancelled for political reasons. As Mother Teresa was much less of a political figure than the Pope she obviously had more freedom to travel and considered nowhere off-limits. A government might be Islamic, Buddhist, Orthodox or atheistic – it made no odds to her.

THE LETTERS

In Lucinda Vardey's *Mother Teresa: A Simple Path*, Mother Teresa is quoted as saying, 'God is everywhere and in everything and without him we cannot exist. I have never for one moment doubted the existence of God but I know some people do.'[2] That was exactly the kind of comment most people expected from her.

Right from her early days in Calcutta, she had repeatedly asked that her letters be destroyed, feeling that they put the spotlight on herself rather than God. Archbishop Perier told her that they were the property of the congregation. In 1999, the Jesuits in Calcutta submitted her letters and diaries to Father Kolodiejchuk, who was in charge of gathering evidence for her canonization. When he published some of them in *The Journal of Theological Reflection*, a Jesuit publication in India, in 2001, a new side of her was revealed for the first time. In her writings, she spoke of interior darkness, of feeling unloved by God and of wondering if he really existed.

Because the letters appeared at the same time as the terrorist attack on the World Trade Center, they attracted scant media coverage. For some reason, there was also very little interest the following year when the Rome on-line news agency Zenit published four instalments of her writings entitled *The Soul of Mother Teresa: Hidden Aspects of Her Interior Life*.

This was not the case in 2007 when Father Kolodiejchuk published a collection of her letters and writings in *Mother Teresa: Come Be My Light*. This time, they caused a sensation in the media, leading to headlines such as 'Letters reveal Mother Teresa tormented by questions of faith' in *The Times*, 'The Secret Life of Mother Teresa', splashed across a glum-looking photo of her on the cover of *TIME* magazine, and the even more sensational 'Did Mother Teresa Believe in God?' in the *Daily Mail*. The Spanish newspaper *Ideal* was more restrained. 'Teresa of Calcutta spent her last 50 years steeped in spiritual crisis,' said its headline. Many postings on the internet posed the same question as the *Daily Mail*: was she an atheist? The Italian newspaper *La Repubblica* carried an interview with Spanish Cardinal Julian Herranz, a member of the Congregation for the Causes of Saints, who made it clear that the revelations would not in any way damage her cause for canonization.

And Christians seemed to be just as surprised to learn of her inner battles. Television producer Mary Rose Bacani, who made a documentary about Mother Teresa in 2005, probably spoke for many when she said that, before the letters were published, she had just seen her as an old lady who was very holy. Reading about her struggles in faith had made her more real and easy to relate to.

The response from Christians elsewhere was summed up best by a cartoon in the US magazine *Christianity Today*. It depicted a newsreader saying: 'In other news, people of faith were shocked to learn that a woman who devoted her entire life to chastity, poverty and caring for lepers had experienced some bad days...'

Father Jonathan Moores, Fox News Channel's religious correspondent in Rome, tried to put the record straight: 'You could never have done what Mother Teresa did for all those years if you didn't have faith. And this is the difference. Did Mother Teresa have doubts on a human level about her faith? Of course she did. All of us do. But did she give in to these temptations of doubt on a spiritual, theological level? No she didn't.'

In an interview with Vatican Radio, Father Raniero Cantalamessa, an Italian priest who is known as the pope's preacher, suggested that her dark night of the soul – her feeling of God's absence in her prayer – prevented her from ever falling into the trap of succumbing to the kind of adulation much of the media showered upon her as a living saint.

The publication of *Come Be My Light* roused Christopher Hitchens once more, who claimed in an article in *Newsweek* that the letters proved Mother Teresa didn't believe in God and her life had been a charade.

He was wrong. What the letters and diary entries actually revealed was not a lack of faith but a blind faith. The darkness that Mother Teresa endured was a common feature in the lives of mystics. Spanish Carmelite St John of the Cross, Mother Teresa's namesake, the French Carmelite St Thérèse of Lisieux, and St Jane Frances Chantal, founder of the Visitation Sisters, were just some of those who experienced intense spiritual darkness throughout much of their lives. As Father Kolodiejchuk was at pains to point out, 'a crisis of faith is one thing; a trial of faith is another thing'.[3]

St Vincent de Paul said of Jane Frances: 'She was full of faith, yet all her life had been tormented by thoughts against it.' He could have just as easily been writing about Mother Teresa. Those who seized on the letters as evidence that she didn't actually believe in God merely demonstrated their ignorance of the complex nature of faith and of leading a spiritual life.

Father Benedict Groeschel, who co-founded the radical Franciscan Friars of the Renewal, got to know Mother Teresa well during her many visits to New York. He recalled, 'While she experienced that darkness, I would be giving a holy hour at four o'clock in the afternoon in the blazing summer heat in the South Bronx, in that little house the sisters lived in, and Mother would be in the most profound prayer.'[4] He went as far as to suggest that she was a prophetess, meaning not that she saw into the future, but that she told the truth when people didn't want to hear it.

SUFFERING

The question of how to reconcile a loving God with suffering is one that many ask and one that theologians have grappled with down the centuries.

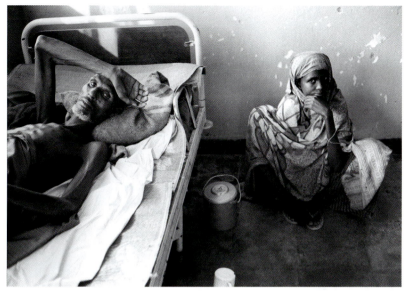

Despite the doubts that haunted Mother Teresa, she seems never to have found any contradiction between a loving God and the existence of suffering. And she had seen more suffering than most: from emaciated men and women in her homes for the dying in India and Aids patients in New York to anguished faces of famine in Ethiopia and terrified mentally disabled children in war-torn Beirut. Her response when asked about suffering was that it was not God, but human beings misusing their free will who were ultimately responsible. She once said, 'When a poor person dies of hunger, it has not happened because God did not take care of him or her. It has happened because neither you nor I wanted to give that person what he or she needed. We have refused to be instruments of love in the hands of God to give the poor a piece of bread, to offer them a dress with which to ward off the cold.'[5]

Her spiritual struggle taught her that no matter what finely honed theological sound bites the church used to explain the Christian faith, in the end God was a mystery. She liked to tell the famous story of the time St Augustine of Hippo encountered a boy trying to fill a hole with water. When St Augustine told him it was impossible, he replied, 'It is still easier to put the ocean into this hole than for you to understand the mystery of God.'

And when speaking about poverty, she always pointed out that

Rather than a place of compassion, the home was made to look like a place of cruelty. This was not hard to achieve given the challenging and difficult work that faced the sisters.

the world also suffered from spiritual poverty, something few would have guessed she experienced herself. 'Sometimes people can hunger for more than bread. It is possible that our children, our husband, our wife, do not hunger for bread, do not need clothes, do not lack a house. But are we equally sure that none of them feels alone, abandoned, neglected, needing some affection? That, too, is poverty.'[6]

MORE CRITICISM

After her death, the criticisms of the Missionaries of Charity continued. A television documentary in 2001 and an article in the German magazine *Stern* both alleged that the congregation had failed to provide proper accounting. In 2005, undercover reporter Donal McIntyre passed himself off as a volunteer and spent a week secretly filming at the Daya Dan home for physically and mentally disabled children in Calcutta. When his film was broadcast in the UK on Channel 5 it presented a picture of children being neglected and badly treated by the sisters and volunteers. Rather than a place of compassion, the home was made to look like a place of cruelty. This was not hard to achieve given the challenging and difficult work that faced the sisters.

In response to the film, Sister Nirmala said that his allegations would be treated seriously, explaining that physical restraints are used only when absolutely necessary for the safety of the child and for limited periods of time.

There was controversy of a different kind when Hillary Clinton used an image of Mother Teresa in her 2008 campaign to be the Democrats' presidential candidate. The footage of Hillary Clinton waving alongside

Mother Teresa was immediately followed by a clip of her speaking at the 1995 International Conference on Women in Beijing, saying, 'It is no longer acceptable to discuss women's rights as separate from human rights.'[7] After a request from the Missionaries of Charity, it was removed.

REVOLUTIONARY

While some of the methods Mother Teresa adopted in her homes could be called anachronistic, she was a trailblazer in other areas. Although the Vatican II document *Nostra Aetate* had acknowledged that other religions 'reflect a ray of truth that enlightens all men', it wasn't until Pope John Paul II burst on the scene that the Catholic Church pushed interfaith dialogue towards the top of its agenda. His gathering of the leaders from the world's religions in Assisi in 1986 marked a new attitude in the Vatican to other faiths.

Yet right from the first days of the Missionaries of Charity, Mother Teresa was living out interfaith dialogue through the way she worked with Hindus, Muslims and others. She once said, 'There is only one God and He is God to all, therefore it is important that everyone is seen as equal before God. I've always said we should help a Hindu become a better Hindu, a Muslim become a better Muslim, a Catholic become a better Catholic.'[8]

At the same time, she always made it clear that she wanted everyone to come to know Jesus. She had only to look at the tiny Christian presence scattered around in India to know this was unlikely to happen. She spoke more of converting hearts, once saying, 'Not even Almighty God can convert a person unless that person wants it.'[9]

Despite her openness to what was good in other faiths, she steered clear of the course adopted by theologians in Asia, such as Father Tissa Balasuriya, a Sri Lankan member of the Oblates of Mary Immaculate, and Belgian Jesuit Father Jaques Dupuis, both of whom ran into Vatican opposition for their interpretation of Catholic doctrine.

And long before the environment became an issue of primary importance for politicians and others in the West, Mother Teresa had set up projects where women earned a living by making bags for shops from recycled paper. Not only that, but in her houses she wasted nothing and made sure that her sisters lived simply and frugally. When a reporter once asked her if she ever got angry or frustrated, she replied, 'Yes, I get angry sometimes when I see waste, when things that are wasted are what people need, things that could save them from dying. Frustrated? No, never.'[10]

STYLE

Mother Teresa responded to immediate needs, such as in Bangladesh, Ethiopia or Armenia. It was for others to tackle the causes of poverty. In other words, she concentrated on aid rather than development. On a visit in 1988 to Khayelitsha, a black township in South Africa, she was asked what service her sisters could offer. She replied, 'I cannot give you that answer until I talk to people. Only then can I see with my own eyes and give them my love.'[11]

She didn't work through committees, sub-committees, feasibility studies, draft proposals, reports, or any of the other methods that are usually a feature of aid agencies and charities. When she came across

> *'While others talk, she works. While others put questions, she solves problems. She has a sense of the real, of the urgent. She sees a need and fills it on the spot.'*

suffering, she responded immediately, figuring that she would work out the details later.

A Missionaries of Charity brother once said, 'Her activity is amazing. While others talk, she works. While others put questions, she solves problems. She has a sense of the real, of the urgent. She sees a need and fills it on the spot.'[12]

For Mother Teresa it was essential for action to be accompanied by prayer. In his first encyclical, *Deus Caritas Est* ('God is Love'), Pope Benedict XVI said, 'In the example of Blessed Teresa of Calcutta we have a clear illustration of the fact that time devoted to God in prayer not only does not detract from effective and loving service to our neighbour but is in fact the inexhaustible source of that service.'[13]

CELEBRITY

It was the media who, to a large extent, created the image of Mother Teresa as a living saint. Hitchens had a point when he said, 'The rich world has a poor conscience. It wants in fact it needs to think that someone somewhere is doing something about the third world.'[14]

Gezim Alpion in his book *Mother Teresa: Saint or Celebrity?* says that Mother Teresa was, like all celebrities, a brand. 'Mother Teresa's work among the poor and her spirituality are and will remain for some time to come one of the Vatican's most remarkable charity and spiritual brands in an age when, like any other religion, Roman Catholicism is striving hard to play a more active and influential role in the lives of the faithful and to make new converts.'[15]

It's true, Mother Teresa was a celebrity. But she was celebrated for doing extraordinary acts and making the world a better place. She was not celebrated, like so many people who appear in the media nowadays, for being famous for no other reason than her looks, for being outrageous, or for promoting her own ego. She was celebrated for holding up to us an ideal of love and compassion that we all, deep down, subscribe to but most of the time cannot live up to.

It's because of this that she has continued to fascinate us long after her death. In 2003, English actress Olivia Hussey (who had played the Virgin Mary in the Franco Zeffirelli television epic *Jesus of Nazareth*) played her in a movie made for Italian television. To coincide with her beatification, a film festival was held in Calcutta at which films from Lebanon, Japan, Spain, India, Canada and the US were shown. In 2006, playwright Arun Kuckreja brought her life to the stage in India. The following year, the tenth anniversary of her death, saw two more plays. In Minnesota, USA, *The Diana Story* explored her relationship with Princess Diana, while in England, *The Bargain* brought to the stage her meeting with tycoon Robert Maxwell in 1988. In Rome, her life was celebrated in a musical. Elsewhere, in Skopje, the city of her birth, and Calcutta, the city she adopted, statues of her were unveiled.

In his autobiography *The Road Taken*, BBC reporter Michael Buerk, who brought back those harrowing scenes from Ethiopia, recalled meeting her in Calcutta. 'I met Mother Teresa and saw a shrunken old woman,

A woman touches the sculpture of Mother Teresa in Skopje, 5 September 2007, on the tenth anniversary of her death. Mother Teresa, was born in Skopje, and died in Kolkata on 5 September 1997, at the age of 87.

focused to the point of obsession on her way of helping the poor. There were those, even then, who questioned her motives, her austere and narrow methods, and her results. But the force of her character seemed to burst out of her wrinkled old body and wizened face – an extraordinary woman even if she was not a saint.'[16]

It is certain that the Vatican will declare her a saint (as one American priest commented, 'she was like the gospel in technicolour'). And, of course, for some she had been a saint for many years, the knowledge of which must have made her very uncomfortable, for she knew her own faults well. It is sometimes said that those in the church who are engaged in social justice lack spirituality, while those who focus on spirituality lack social justice. With all her faults, Mother Teresa was the full ticket, putting her concerns for social justice into concrete action and ensuring every moment of her life was in pursuit of God. That was the secret of her appeal to so many.

Endnotes

Introduction

1. Kenneth Woodward, *The Wall Street Journal*, September 8, 2007

Chapter 1

1. David Porter, *Mother Teresa: The Early Years*, p. 13
2. Eileen Egan, *Such a Vision of the Street*, p. 8
3. *The Story of a Soul by St Thérèse of Lisieux*, page unknown
4. David Porter, *Mother Teresa: The Early Years*, p. 29
5. *Ibid*, p. 32

Chapter 2

1. David Porter, *Mother Teresa: The Early Years*, p. 37
2. *Ibid*, p. 40
3. *Ibid*, p. 48
4. *Ibid*, p. 56
5. Brian Kolodiejchuk, *Mother Teresa: Come Be My Light*, p. 98
6. *Ibid*, p. 96
7. *Ibid*, p. 99

Chapter 3

1. Eileen Egan, *Such a Vision of the Street*, p. 40
2. David Porter, *Mother Teresa: The Early Years*, p. 73
3. *Ibid*, p. 76
4. Desmond Doig, *Mother Teresa: Her People and Her Work*, p. 40

5. David Porter, *Mother Teresa: The Early Years*, p. 79

6. Eileen Egan, *Such a Vision of the Street*, p. 50

7. *Ibid*

8. Brian Kolodiejchuk, *Mother Teresa: Come Be My Light*, p. 164

9. Source unknown

10. Source unknown

Chapter 4

1. Source unknown

2. Brian Kolodiejchuk, *Mother Teresa: Come Be My Light*, p. 187

3. Eileen Egan, *Such a Vision of the Street*, p. 145

4. Brian Kolodiejchuk, *Mother Teresa: Come Be My Light*, p. 210

5. *Ibid*, p. 212

6. *Ibid*, p. 214

7. *Ibid*, p. 230

8. Kathryn Spink, *Mother Teresa: An Authorized Biography*, p. 112

9. E. Le Joly, *We Do It for Jesus*, p. 69

10. Malcolm Muggeridge, *Something Beautiful for God*, p. 41

11. Eileen Egan, *Such a Vision of the Street*, p. 235

12. Anne Sebba, *Mother Teresa: Beyond the Image*, p. 80

Chapter 5

1. E. Le Joly, *We Do It for Jesus*, p. 153

2. Source unknown

3. Jose Luis Gonzalez-Balado (ed.), *Mother Teresa: In My Own Words*, p. 35

4. Kathryn Spink, *Mother Teresa: An Authorized Biography*, p. 87

5. Eileen Egan, *Such a Vision of the Street*, p. 230

6. Anne Sebba, *Mother Teresa: Beyond the Image*, p. 93

7. *Ibid*

8. Lucinda Vardey (ed.), *Mother Teresa: A Simple Path* p. 43–44

9. *Ibid*, p. 43

10. E. Le Joly, *We Do It for Jesus*, p. 10

11. Eileen Egan, *Such a Vision of the Street*, p. 458

12. E. Le Joly, *We Do It for Jesus*, p. 11

13. Brian Kolodiejchuk, *Mother Teresa: Come Be My Light*

14. *Time* magazine, December 4, 1989

15. www.nobelprize.org

16. Eileen Egan, *Such a Vision of the Street*, p. 389

17. www.nobelprize.org

18. *Ibid*

Chapter 6

1. Brian Kolodiejchuk, *Mother Teresa: Come Be My Light*, p. 294

2. Anne Sebba, *Mother Teresa: Beyond the Image*, p. 233

3. *New York Times*, August 15, 1983

4. Eileen Egan, *Such a Vision of the Street*, p. 441

5. Kathryn Spink, *Mother Teresa: An Authorized Biography*, pp. 208, 205

6. *Ibid*, p. 205

7. E. Le Joly, *We Do It for Jesus*, p. 12

8. Father Charles O'Connor, *Classic Catholic Converts*, p. 192

9. BBC TV news report

10. Anne Sebba, *Mother Teresa: Beyond the Image*, p. 115

11. George Weigel, *Witness to Hope*, p. 566

12. Lucinda Vardey (ed.), *Mother Teresa: A Simple Path*, p. 34

13. *Time* magazine, December 4, 1989

Chapter 7

1. Anne Sebba, *Mother Teresa: Beyond the Image*, p. 117

2. TV news footage: source unknown

3. www.ewtn.com

4. www.priestsforlife.org

5. *Ibid*

6. *Ibid*

7. Hillary Rodham Clinton, *Living History*, p. 418

8. *Ibid*

9. Source unknown

10. Lucinda Vardey (ed.), *Mother Teresa: A Simple Path*, p. 71

11. Mother Teresa's address to the UN Conference on Women in Beijing, 1995

12. Lucinda Vardey (ed.), *Mother Teresa: A Simple Path*. p. 53

13. E. Le Joly, *We Do It for Jesus*, p. 90

Chapter 8

1. *The Nation*, 1992

2. *Hell's Angel* documentary, Channel 4, 1994

3. *Ibid*

4. *Ibid*

5. Source unknown

6. *Hell's Angel* documentary, Channel 4, 1994

7. Source unknown

8. Aroup Chatterjee, *Mother Teresa: The Final Verdict*, p. 200

9. Anne Sebba, *Mother Teresa: Beyond the Image*, p. 136

10. Aroup Chatterjee, *Mother Teresa: The Final Verdict*, p. 202

11. Anne Sebba, *Mother Teresa: Beyond the Image*, pp. 142–3

12. Source unknown

13. *The Tablet*, November 11, 1994

14. Source unknown

Chapter 9

1. Anne Sebba, *Mother Teresa: Beyond the Image*, p. 245

2. Lucinda Vardey, *Mother Teresa: A Simple Path*, p. 77

3. Father Benedict Groeschel on EWTN, date unknown

Chapter 10

1. George Weigel, *Witness to Hope*, p. 513

2. Lucinda Vardey, *Mother Teresa: A Simple Path*, p. 65

3. Brian Kolodiejchuk, *Mother Teresa: Come Be My Light*

4. EWTN TV programme, date unknown

5. Jose Luis Gonzalez-Balado (ed.), *Mother Teresa: In My Own Words*, p. 25

6. *Ibid*, p. 27

7. *Independent Catholic News*, June 21, 2007

8. Lucinda Vardey, *Mother Teresa: A Simple Path*, p. 55

9. Desmond Doig, *Mother Teresa: Her People and Her Work*, p. 136

10. Eileen Egan, *Such a Vision of the Street*, p. 297

11. *New York Times*, November 9, 1988

12. E. Le Joly, *We Do It for Jesus*, p. 90

13. Pope Benedict XVI, *Deus Caritas Est*, pp. 31, 68

14. *Hell's Angel* documentary, Channel 4, 1994

15. Gezim Alpion, *Mother Teresa: Saint or Celebrity?*, p. 234
16. Michael Buerk, *The Road Taken*, p. 339

Bibliography

Gezim Alpion, *Mother Teresa: Saint or Celebrity?*, Routledge, 2007.

Michael Buerk, *The Road Taken*, Arrow Books Ltd, 2005.

Aroup Chatterjee, *Mother Teresa: The Final Verdict*, Meteor Books, 2003.

Hillary Rodham Clinton, *Living History*, Headline, 2003.

Desmond Doig, *Mother Teresa: Her People and Her Work*, Fount, 1978.

Eileen Egan, *Such a Vision of the Street, Mother Teresa: The Spirit and the Work*, Sidgwick & Jackson, 1985.

Jose Luis Gonzalez-Balado (ed.), *Mother Teresa: In My Own Words*, Gramercy Books, 1996.

Georges Gorree and Jean Barbier, *For the Love of God: Mother Teresa of Calcutta*, T. Shand Alba Publications, 1974.

Christopher Hitchens, *The Missionary Position: Mother Teresa in Theory and Practice*, Verso, 1995.

Michael Hollings, *Thérèse of Lisieux*, Fount, 1981.

E. Le Joly, *We Do It for Jesus: Mother Teresa and Her Missionaries of Charity*, Darton, Longman & Todd, 1977.

Brian Kolodiejchuk, *Mother Teresa: Come Be My Light – The Private Writings of the Saint of Calcutta*, Doubleday, 2007.

James McGovern, *To Give the Love of Christ: A Portrait of Mother Teresa and the Missionaries of Charity*, Paulist Press, 1978.

Malcolm Muggeridge, *Something Beautiful for God*, Collins, 1971.

Father Eugene Palumbi, SDB, *Mother Teresa: Angel of God*, Resurrection Press, 2000.

David Porter, *Mother Teresa: The Early Years*, SPCK, 1986.

Anne Sebba, *Mother Teresa: Beyond the Image*, Orion, 1997.

G. D. Solomon, *Brothers of Mother Teresa*, St Paul Publications, 1987.

Kathryn Spink, *Mother Teresa: An Authorized Biography*, Fount, 1998.

Kathryn Spink and Jose Luis Gonzalez-Balado, *Spirit of Bethlehem: Brother Andrew and the Missionary Brothers of Charity*, SPCK, 1987.

Mother Teresa and Brother Roger, *Prayer: Seeking the Heart of God*, Fount, 1992.

Lucinda Vardey (ed.), *Mother Teresa: A Simple Path*, Rider, 1995.

Father Sebastian Vazhakala, MC, *Life With Mother Teresa, My Thirty-Year Friendship with the Mother of the Poor*, Servant Books, 2004.

George Weigel, *Witness to Hope: The Biography of Pope John Paul II*, Cliff Street Books/ HarperCollins, 1999.

Sam Wellman, *Mother Teresa: Missionary of Charity*, Barbour, 1997.

Index

Picture Acknowledgments

Alamy: pp 19 Mary Evans Picture Library; 22 Profimedia International s.r.o.; 25 Tibor Bognar; 47 Sean Sprague; 76 Terry Fincher, Photo Int

Corbis: pp 3 Kapoor Baldev/Sygma; 30 Michael Maslan Historic Photographs; 52 Frèdèric Soltan/Sygma; 62, 148 Jayanta Shaw/Reuters; 74, 86, 101 Bettmann; 83 Philippe Caron/Sygma; 103 Arnaud de Wildenberg/Sygma; 117 Michel Setboun; 125 Robert Maass; 157 Bernard Bisson/Sygma; 162 Peter Turnley; 164 Amet Jean Pierre/Sygma

Getty: pp 27, 57 Time & Life Pictures; 79 Leon Morris; 91, 134 Tim Graham; 96 Keystone; 98 Luc Novovitch/AFP; 104 David Rubinger/Time Life Pictures; 107 AFP; 115 Francois Lochon; 131 Joyce Naltchayan/AFP; 140 David Levenson; 143 David Ake/AFP; 144 Gemma Levine/Hulton Archive; 154 Anwar Hussein; 159 Raveendran/AFP; 160 Pablo Bartholomew; 168 Franco Origlia; 173 Joel Robine/AFP; 178 Robert Atanasovski/AFP

Jon Arnold Images: p 13

Magnum: pp 42, 51, 58 Raghu Rai/Magnum Photos

Photographers Direct: p 119 Mark Goebel

Topfoto: pp 15 Topham Picturepoint © 2001; 16 World History Archive/TopFoto; 17, 41 Topham Picturepoint © 2002; 28 TopFoto © 2005; 32 Topham Picturepoint © 2003; 37 Dinodia/Topham © 2004; 46 Roger-Viollet © 2005; 112 AP/Topham © 2003; 69 Topfoto © 2005; 122 AP/Topham © 2001

Lion Hudson

Commissioning editor: Kate Kirkpatrick

Project editors: Catherine Sinfield, Miranda Powell

Designer: Nicholas Rous

Picture researcher: Kate Leech

Production manager: Kylie Ord